T0332212

Darkweb Cyber Threat Intelligence Mining

The important and rapidly emerging new field known as "cyber threat intelligence" explores the paradigm that defenders of computer networks gain a better understanding of their adversaries by understanding what assets they have available for an attack. In this book, a team of experts examines a new type of cyber threat intelligence from the heart of the malicious hacking underworld—the darkweb. These highly secure sites have allowed anonymous communities of malicious hackers to exchange ideas, techniques, and buy/sell malware and exploits.

Aimed at both cybersecurity practitioners and researchers, this book represents a first step toward a better understanding of malicious hacking communities on the darkweb and what to do about them. The authors examine real-world darkweb data through a combination of human and automated techniques to gain insight into these communities, describing both methodology and results.

JOHN ROBERTSON is a student at Arizona State University pursuing undergraduate degrees in both Computer Science and Electrical Engineering where his work has been nominated for the Computing Research Association's Outstanding Undergraduate Researcher award. He is a recipient of an ARO Undergraduate Research Apprenticeship Program grant as well as two Fulton Undergraduate Research Initiative grants for his work involving the application of artificial intelligence techniques to cybersecurity problems in the Cyber-Socio Intelligent System Laboratory with Dr. Paulo Shakarian. John also has industry experience as a software engineering intern with Microsoft on the Windows Core Development team.

AHMAD DIAB is a Computer Engineering Ph.D. student at Arizona State University. His current work in the Cyber-Socio Intelligent System Laboratory focuses on the application of AI techniques to cybersecurity problems. Ahmad is a recipient of SIPGA award from ASTAR agency, Singapore. Previously, he was a Java developer at EtQ compliance Company. Ahmad holds a B.S. in computer engineering from Jordan University of Science and Technology.

ERICSSON MARIN is a Computer Science Ph.D. Student at Arizona State University. He works at the Cyber-Socio Intelligent System Laboratory under the guidance of Dr. Paulo Shakarian, with research projects at the intersection of Social Network Analysis, AI and Cybersecurity. He received his M.Sc. in Computer Science from Federal University of Goias, Brazil, and has published numerous papers in the area of social network analysis. He also has real-world experience as a software designer managing different software factories. In 2015, Ericsson was awarded with a Brazilian Science Without Borders scholarship to pursue his Ph.D.

ERIC NUNES is a Ph.D. student in the computer engineering program at Arizona State University. His research focuses on the intelligence techniques to cybersecurity problems. Previously, Eric was a Research Associate at the Brain Engineering Lab at Dartmouth College. Eric holds an M.S. in Electrical Engineering from Syracuse University, New York.

VIVIN PALIATH is a Computer Science Ph.D. student at Arizona State University. His research at ASU focuses on the application of artificial intelligence and game-theoretic techniques to cybersecurity problems. Vivin received both his B.S. in Computer Engineering and M.S. in Computer Science from Arizona State University. He has more than a decade of industry experience and is also currently working as a Senior Software Engineer at Infusionsoft, a company that develops marketing-automation software for small businesses.

JANA SHAKARIAN is a research scientist at Arizona State University and has been researching malicious hacking groups and their online activity since 2012. She has coauthored two books, *Introduction to Cyber-Warfare* and *Computational Analysis of Terrorist Groups: Lashkar-e-Taiba*. She holds M.A. degrees in Sociology and Cultural and Social Anthropology from the Johannes Gutenberg University, Mainz, Germany. Previously, she was a staff social scientist for the University of Maryland Institute for Advanced Computer Studies where she worked with computer scientists on the cultural modeling of non-state armed actors and the interpretation of nonverbal communication.

PAULO SHAKARIAN is an Assistant Professor at Arizona State University's School of Computing, Informatics, and Decision Support Engineering where he directs the Cyber-Socio Intelligent System Laboratory, specializing in cyber-security, social network analysis, and AI. He has written numerous articles in scientific journals and has authored several books, including *Introduction to Cyber-Warfare: A Multidisciplinary Approach*. His work has been featured in news outlets such as *The Economist, Popular Science*, and *WIRED*. He is a recipient of the Air Force Young Investigator Award, Fulton Entrepreneurial Professor award, MIT Technology Review's "Best of 2013," and the DARPA Service Chiefs' Fellowship.

Darkweb Cyber Threat
Intelligence Mining

JOHN ROBERTSON, AHMAD DIAB,
ERICSSON MARIN, ERIC NUNES, VIVIN PALIATH,
JANA SHAKARIAN, AND PAULO SHAKARIAN
Arizona State University

CAMBRIDGE
UNIVERSITY PRESS

University Printing House, Cambridge CB2 8BS, United Kingdom

One Liberty Plaza, 20th Floor, New York, NY 10006, USA

477 Williamstown Road, Port Melbourne, VIC 3207, Australia

314-321, 3rd Floor, Plot 3, Splendor Forum, Jasola District Centre, New Delhi - 110025, India

79 Anson Road, #06-04/06, Singapore 079906

Cambridge University Press is part of the University of Cambridge.

It furthers the University's mission by disseminating knowledge in the pursuit of education, learning and research at the highest international levels of excellence.

www.cambridge.org
Information on this title: www.cambridge.org/9781107185777
DOI: 10.1017/9781316888513

© John Robertson, Ahmad Diab, Ericsson Marin, Eric Nunes, Vivin Paliath, Jana Shakarian, and Paulo Shakarian 2017

First published 2017

A catalogue record for this publication is available from the British Library

ISBN 978-1-107-18577-7 Hardback

Contents

Foreword

A human activity undergoes "industrialization" when it adopts systematic means for the creation, production, and distribution of goods. A key ingredient of industrialization is the division of labor—including the specialization of basic research, commercialization, and end-user delivery and support. The net effect of industrialization is a profound amplification of both technology development and production capacity, typically leading to broader distribution and consumption of the underlying goods.

Darkweb Cyber Threat Intelligence Mining is the first principled study of the ongoing industrialization of cyber offense. It exposes the extent to which malware and associated attacker technologies have become commodity goods that are globally produced, marketed, distributed, and consumed.

Like eBay and Amazon, the darkweb is an online marketplace that brings cyber offense developers, buyers, and middlemen together. However, unlike eBay and Amazon, the darkweb is deliberately difficult to access and interpret by the outsider. The authors make a valuable contribution to the cyber defense community by describing a variety of technologies and techniques they have developed and used to penetrate the otherwise opaque cyber offense industrial base. As such, this book represents a seminal step toward leveling the cyber playing field. Because cybersecurity pits the creativity, knowledge, and technology of defenders against those of the attackers, each player must make great effort to understand and exploit the strengths and weakness of the other players. Cyber-attackers have had a decided edge in this respect for many years. Targeted applications and operating systems are easy to obtain and reverse engineer. Virtually all defensive technologies are open source or commercially available. Cyber defense research and deployment advances are widely published, promoted, and taught.

Thanks to the determined efforts of the authors and the documentation of their work in *Darkweb Cyber Threat Intelligence Mining*, we are for the first time able to shine persistent light on the emerging technologies and capabilities of cyber-attackers.

Many of us try to understand why, despite the increasing investments in cyber defense research and products, cybersecurity remains a huge, and possibly growing, challenge. I can't help but think that a significant reason is that the offensive community has been quietly and covertly industrializing itself at a pace that defenders have not fully appreciated. Without visibility into that industrial base, defenders do not know what is in the production pipeline and cannot properly prepare. They can only react, as has traditionally been the case. This book might change that.

Darkweb Cyber Threat Intelligence Mining represents a tipping point in cyber security. It is a must-read for anyone involved in the modern cyber struggle.

George Cybenko
Dartmouth College
Grantham, NH, USA
August 29, 2016

Preface

Rapidly emerging is an exciting new field known as "cyber threat intelligence." The key idea with this paradigm is that defenders of computer networks gain a better understanding of their adversaries by analyzing what assets they have available for an attack. In this book, we examine a new type of cyber threat intelligence that takes one into the heart of the malicious hacking underworld— the darkweb. These highly secure sites have allowed for an anonymous community of malicious hackers to exchange ideas, techniques, and buy/sell malware and exploits. This book examines how we explored this problem through a combination of human and automated techniques to grasp a better understanding of this community. We describe both methodology and some of the resulting insights. This book serves as a first step toward a better understanding of malicious hacking communities on the darkweb.

The authors would like to acknowledge the generous support from the Arizona State University Global Security Initiative (GSI), the Office of Naval Research Neptune program, the Arizona State University Institute for Social Science Research (ISSR), and CNPq-Brazil, which have enabled our research in the area of cyber threat intelligence mined from the darkweb. Specific individuals, we would like to thank include Jamie Winterton, Nadya Bliss, H. Russel Bernard, William Brandt, Andrew Gunn, Robert Morgus, Frank Grimmelmann, Amanda Thart, and Vineet Mishra. We also would like to extend a special thanks to Lauren Cowels, our editor at Cambridge University Press, whose assistance throughout the creation of this book was much appreciated.

1

Introduction

Recently, the online market for exploit kits, malware, botnet rentals, tutorials, and other hacking products has continued to evolve, and what was once a rather hard-to-penetrate and exclusive market—whose buyers were primarily western governments [95]—has now become more accessible to a much wider population. Specifically, the darknet—portions of the Internet accessible through anonymization protocols such as Tor and i2p—has become populated with a variety of markets specializing in such products [94, 2]. In particular, 2015 saw the introduction of darknet markets specializing in zero-day exploit kits, designed to leverage previously undiscovered vulnerabilities. These exploit kits are difficult and time consuming to develop—and often are sold at premium prices.

The explosive increase in popularity of exploit markets and hacker forums presents a valuable opportunity to cyber defenders. These online communities provide a new source of information about potential adversaries, consequently forming the nascent cyber threat intelligence industry. Pre-reconnaissance cyber threat intelligence refers to information gathered prior to a malicious actor interacting with a defended computer system. To provide a concrete example demonstrating the importance of pre-reconnaissance cyber threat intelligence, consider the case study shown in Table 1.1. A Microsoft Windows vulnerability was identified in February 2015. Microsoft's public press release regarding this vulnerability was essentially their way of warning customers of a security flaw. At the time of its release, there was no publicly known method to leverage this flaw in a cyber-attack (i.e., an available exploit). However, about a month later, an exploit was found to be on sale in a darknet exploit marketplace. It was not until July when FireEye, a major cybersecurity firm, identified that the Dyre Banking Trojan, designed to steal credit card information, exploited this particular vulnerability. This vignette illustrates how threat warnings gathered from the darknet can provide valuable information for security

1

Table 1.1. *Exploit example*

Timeline	Event
February 2015	Microsoft identifies Windows vulnerability MS15-010/CVE 2015-0057 for remote code execution. There was no publicly known exploit at the time the vulnerability was released.
April 2015	An exploit for MS15-010/CVE 2015-0057 was found on a darknet market on sale for 48 BTC (around $10,000–15,000 at the time).
July 2015	FireEye identified that the Dyre Banking Trojan, designed to steal credit card number, actually exploited this vulnerability.[1]

professionals in the form of early-warning threat indicators. Between Dyre and the similar Dridex banking trojan, nearly 6 out of every 10 global organizations were affected, a shocking statistic.[2]

In another instance, 17-year-old hacker Sergey Taraspov from St. Petersburg, Russia, along with a small team of hackers, allegedly wrote a piece of malware that targeted point-of-sale (POS) software and sold it for $2,000 on a Russian forum-cum-marketplace. This malware was, in turn, used by around forty individuals to steal over 110 million American credit card numbers in the "Target" data breach of 2013.[3]

It is now possible, and quite common, to leverage data-mining and machine-learning techniques to make sense out of large quantities of data. After further motivating the importance of cyber threat intelligence and discussing online hacker communities in detail, we will discuss specifically how data-mining and machine-learning techniques can be applied to the cyber threat intelligence domain. Using these techniques, we will be able to gain additional insight into the structure of online hacker communities as well as the behavior of individuals within them. We will also draw from the artificial intelligence literature to build threat models, informed from the data mined from hacker communities, to provide system-specific cyber intelligence.

This book is intended to give an overarching view into the burgeoning field of cyber threat intelligence. The remainder of the book is structured as follows: Chapter 2 will further motivate the use of cyber threat intelligence by organizations, discussing and addressing some of the difficulties in realizing wide-scale cyber threat intelligence adoption. Chapter 3, will discuss, in detail, the online

---

[1] https://www.fireeye.com/blog/threat-research/2015/07/dyre_banking_trojan.html

[2] https://www.fireeye.com/blog/threat-research/2015/06/evolution_of_dridex.html

[3] http://www.nbcnews.com/news/world/skilled-cheap-russian-hackers-power-american-cybercrime-n22371

hacker communities from which a lot of cyber threat intelligence is derived. Chapter 4 will introduce techniques to build a large-scale scraping and parsing infrastructure to gather data from darknet communities, discussing some of the associated challenges as well as the performance of various data-mining and machine-learning techniques in the context of gathering cyber threat intelligence. Chapter 5 presents a number of case studies that illustrate how the collected data can be translated to actionable, real-world cyber threat intelligence and uses unsupervised learning techniques to cluster products from darknet markets into specific categories.

The next two chapters (Chapter 6 and 7) introduce more sophisticated models that use the aggregated data from the darknet in interesting ways to provide rich threat intelligence. Chapter 6 frames the host defense scenario as a security game, presenting a game theoretic framework that informs the attacker model with real-world darknet exploit data and is capable of making system-specific policy recommendations. The model presented in Chapter 7 also leverages exploit information, but in the context of defending industrial control systems (ICS): IT infrastructure that controls physical systems (electricity, water, industrial machinery, etc.).

Chapter 8 wraps up the book, discussing ongoing work as well as the unique challenges associated with sociocultural modeling of cyber threat actors and why they necessitate further advances in artificial intelligence—particularly with regard to interdisciplinary efforts with the social sciences.

2

Moving to Proactive Cyber Threat Intelligence

2.1 Introduction

Cybersecurity is often referred to as offense dominant, meaning that the domain generally favors the attacker [67, 65]. The reasoning behind this is simple: a successful defense must block all pathways to a system while a successful attack requires only one. As the old hacker adage goes: "the defender must always be right—the attacker only needs to be right once." This notion of an offense dominant cybersecurity stems directly from "best practices" in the field. These methods primarily rely on technical measures to improve defense. Traditionally these have included variations on patch management, firewall usage, intrusion detection, and antivirus. However, an adversary particularly keen on gaining access to a system can study such defenses with the goal of finding the gaps. These actions are not limited to nation states or large criminal enterprises. The community of malicious hackers is a key enabler for these activities. While important, technical defense measures alone are unlikely to halt attackers and the offense will have the advantage in this case. This chapter explores the use of cyber threat intelligence to address this problem. By gaining insights on the adversary's behavior, we can better address the offense-dominant problem inherent in cybersecurity. The new market for cyber threat intelligence has emerged in recent years due to the realization that technical defensive measures, by themselves, are insufficient to address cybersecurity.

2.1.1 Consider the Threat

Central to the idea of cyber threat intelligence (in its current incarnation) is the sharing of information on the latest observed threats. Such data may be collected by a third party (i.e., a company that specializes in incident response or network monitoring), shared directly between organizations, or shared through a group of organizations (i.e., the various Information Sharing and Analysis Centers or ISACs). Certainly, distribution in a manner that best maximizes such information sharing while respecting the privacy of organizations and individuals is a key concern here, as is the role of government in such arrangements. These are some of several short-term problems that are being addressed by threat intelligence firms today: big data management; identification of attack patterns; sanitization/dissemination of information; knowledge extraction; and others. However, these are all relatively short-term problems. This chapter focuses on a larger, more systemic issue with cyber threat intelligence as it stands today: the vast majority of it is inherently reactive.

Today, most threat intelligence provides awareness on currently employed attack vectors rather than potential attack vectors expected in the future. In other areas focused on security or safety, such as law enforcement and the military, much of what the cybersecurity industry would term threat intelligence would really be considered situational awareness. While enhanced sharing of information is certainly important, the reactive nature of this strategy suggests that it is not a comprehensive solution. Hackers who specialize in finding exploits and building malware platforms continue to improve their craft, especially with regards to how stealthily their malware infects and operates. For example, a study from Symantec found that, on average, zero-days exist "in the wild" for over 300 days before identification [10]. Likewise, in 2016, malware platforms were known to persist on a target system for a median of 146 days before discovery [26].

The rapidly changing threat often causes cybersecurity information and standards to become brittle. To address this, not only must threat behavior be accounted for, but also the future threat landscape. This is likely a contributing factor to the failure of companies providing cyber insurance to accurately predict policy claim amounts [35]. If an auditor assesses an organization's cybersecurity posture based on even the most current best practices and threat signatures, such an assessment will likely become stale in a matter of months. This is due to the simple fact that the threat—the malicious hacker community—is continually evolving. As a community, hackers have a general understanding of the current defense posture, and they make adjustments based on what they discover and perceive. Not accounting for an evolving threat means that actuarial modes based on initial audits rapidly become obsolete as the underlying assumptions soon fail to hold.

2.1.2 The World of the Malicious Hackers: the Deep and Dark Web

It is important to note that the malicious hacking community has grown particularly efficient and agile. One way to gain insight into their activities is to explore malicious hacker forums and marketplaces on the deepweb and darkweb. The deepweb refers to websites accessible through the standard protocols that run most of the world wide web (such as HTTP and HTTPS) but are generally not indexed by major search engines due to security restrictions (such as additional password protection, CAPTCHA's, etc.). It is worth pointing out that the deepweb can just as easily be benign as malicious. The darkweb, on the other hand, refers to sites that use an additional secure protocol that provides further anonymization and/or encryption. Tor is perhaps the best known of such software, but there are others such as i2p and Freenet. With regard to the malicious hacking community, many underground forums and marketplaces have appeared on these parts of the Internet. Forums, like those seen on the open Internet, allow for discussions about various topics. In observing these forums, we have noted that there are often posts by individuals seeking specific hacking needs—"help wanted" posts for cybercrime. Likewise, individuals also post hacker "for hire" advertisements in these communities. We conduct a more thorough exploration of these communities in the next chapter. The economic activity concerning the sale and distribution of items such as malware systems, late-breaking software exploits, and botnets for-rent have led to specialization in the market for malicious hacking products [90]. The malicious community operates as a market—and a very agile one at that—whereas the market for defense is generally rigid. In our research, we have found that vendors of these products often identify certain niche markets. For example, some are focused on creating software exploits that leverage previously unidentified (a.k.a. zero-day) vulnerabilities. Others focus on payload delivery systems–malware that is designed to stealthily evade antivirus software. These platforms are often given the moniker "fully undetectable" or FUD. There are also service providers—who, for a fee, can provide access to botnet infrastructure. This allows the purchaser to conduct large-scale phishing or distributed denial of service (DDoS) attacks. Malicious hackers who specialize are able to better focus on particular products. Specialization also occurs for specific platforms (i.e. mobile vs. desktop) and operating system (Windows vs. Linux). We encountered reason to believe that specialization stems from a hackers's particular skill set, which allows him to bring his products to market in a timely manner in order to fetch higher prices. Later, in Chapter 5, we explore these markets in a quantitative manner. No major operating system or platform seems to be immune, although we can see the digital divide generally replicated. More widely used operating systems and platforms tend to be targeted more often than similar platforms with a smaller userbase. Further enabling the vendors—and also allowing them to focus more on their tradecraft—are marketplace administrators. These individuals run the markets, drive traffic, advertise, and often act as a trusted third party during transactions. Trust is a major issue in such environments. Indeed, through software like Tor and crypto-currencies like Bitcoin, anonymity is generally preserved. This begs an important question: how is trust established? Furthermore, how is a level of trust established that allows for transactions in the tens of thousands of dollars for highly valuable exploits or malware? The amount of money is not trivial, nor is the effort placed in developing many of the products for sale. In our work, we have noted that there is a surprising consistency among usernames across various malicious hacking sites on the deepweb and darkweb [100]. Due to trust-related issues, reputation is very important in these communities. Hundreds of individuals retain the same user name across two or more sites, resulting in a consistent virtual identity that is regularly maintained. These personas actively contribute to online hacking communities providing tutorials, malware samples, and general advice on topics related to criminal hacking and operational security. Since social status within the hacker community is based on meritocracy, hackers need to showcase their cyber-endeavors. In the next three chapters, we illustrate some of these aspects using a data-driven analytical approach. Through these interactions, and the careful maintenance of an anonymous online persona, a malicious hacker can build trust in the community.

2.2 Proactive Intelligence beyond the Deepweb and Darkweb

Using threat intelligence derived from the deepweb and darkweb is one way in which organizations can move toward a more proactive, intelligence-driven cybersecurity. There are also other windows into these types of communities, like social media. Hacking collectives such as Anonymous and LizardSquad often use social media to recruit individual hackers for a campaign [93]. As those involved in such hacking campaigns often consider themselves activists, the term "hacktivism" is often used to describe such activity. Hacktivism campaigns are often planned in the open and are indicative of a pending cyber threat. Many times, these campaigns rely on large numbers of individuals—in many cases lending their machines in a denial of service attack. This was not only seen in campaigns by Anonymous in 2012, but also in groups seeking to contribute in the time of a national conflict, such as Russian youths during the

Russian–Georgian war [96] or Israeli sympathizers during Israel–Hamas conflicts [95]. Another important form of threat intelligence is information gathered by nation states. Such information was rapidly put into action with the swift attribution of the 2015 Sony hack to North Korea by the United States government [32]. The sharing of national-level security intelligence with industry partners is not as far-fetched as it may first seem. In some ways, we already do this with terrorism advisories provided by the Department of Homeland Security and travel advisories and warnings provided by the Department of State. The key is for the information to be sanitized and released in an appropriate manner. The various ISACs previously mentioned provide a trusted community to share such information, and, in some cases, information relating to cybercrime is already shared in this manner. For instance, in Arizona, the nonprofit ACTRA facilitates sharing of law enforcement data with cybersecurity professionals working in the critical infrastructure sector—and similar organizations are copying the ACTRA model in other states. However, any sharing scheme has trade-offs. One of ACTRA's strengths is that it is not itself a government organization—and hence can gain the trust of industry members with relative ease. However, for the same reason, ACTRA will never have the same level of clout within the government as an organization like the NCCIC. Perhaps the way forward is a mix—for example ACTRA has a bi-directional sharing agreement with NCCIC, which is primarily used for the sharing of threat assessments and threat advisories.

2.2.1 Moving Toward a More Proactive Cyber Threat Intelligence

As discussed earlier, the current state-of-the-art for cyber threat intelligence primarily provides information on what is already deployed by would-be cyberattackers. In order to evolve adversarial understanding, we suggest classifying cyber threat intelligence practices. The most basic level would be the aforementioned situational awareness. This would entail situational awareness of one's own enterprise, of peer organizations (i.e., shared through an ISAC), and information obtained from sensors used to gather malicious activities in the wild (i.e., honeypot information). A second level would be the simplest form of proactive intelligence—the identification of an imminent threat to an organization. A prime example of this type of intelligence would be indicators of pending hacktivist activities gained from social media. A third level would be slightly more advanced and forward leaning—understanding a shift in enemy capabilities. This would involve evolving knowledge of what exploits and malware are being developed. The most strategic level of intelligence would comprise a fourth level, in which general knowledge about the malicious hacking

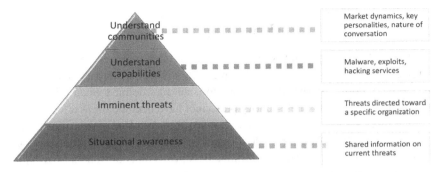

Figure 2.1.   Tiered layers of cyber threat intelligence.

communities is examined. Intelligence at this level would include information about market dynamics within these communities, the rise and fall of particular personalities and venues, the nature of the conversations that take place in the forums, and the overall evolution of these communities. The intuition behind this tiered system (Figure 2.1) is that at the higher levels the information can lead to decisions with progressively more long-term consequences. For example, at the situational awareness (or first) level, the primary action that can be taken is to identify a signature or block an IP address. When a malicious hacker observes a sufficient number of organizations on his target list taking such actions, he changes tactics. Hence, the result is very short term. Likewise, preparing for an imminent cyber campaign (level two) can lead to actions that will cause cyber defenders to make adjustments that last for weeks at a time until, ultimately, the threat actor's campaign comes to an end. An example of a measure for this second level would be the purchase of additional DDoS protection in preparation for a DDoS by a hacker collective. Level three is where decisions start to become more long-term. Identifying ahead of time what software the adversary will develop malware and exploits against can lead to a variety of decisions. These decisions range from deciding to prioritize certain patches, discontinuing use of a piece of software, purchasing or developing software, and segregating certain computers from the rest of the network. Decisions based on fourth-level intelligence are likewise strategic and could lead to decisions on what types of cyber threat intelligence to consume or where an organization places strategic investments in cybersecurity over the long term. Although decisions at the third and fourth level do not provide short-term gains, they are certainly more cost effective in the long run. Making more strategic level decisions based on third and fourth layer intelligence can potentially obviate a large volume of short-term adjustments based on the lower levels.

2.3 Showing Value

An inherent difficulty in marketing cyber threat intelligence is showing value through quantitative metrics. For instance, the number of threats detected in a system could be viewed as a metric, but is success defined when this number increases (showing that security personnel have become more effective in finding threats) or when it decreases (showing that the security measures have prevented threats)? The use of these types of statistics to assess the state of cybersecurity for an organization ultimately depends on context and an overall picture of enemy behavior. If an attack is anticipated (i.e., a hacktivist campaign), a significant number of low-level attacks attempted against an organization should be expected. Likewise, publicity of a successful international law enforcement operation might encourage the expectation of a drop in attacks. For example, in the summer of 2015, law enforcement operation Shrouded Horizon took down the infamous Darkode cybercrime market/forum [81]. In the aftermath, we observed many darkweb hacker marketplaces and communities go offline temporarily, until about six months later Darkode had established a presence on Tor, inviting all former members. Higher-layer threat intelligence further improves the understanding of such numbers. For instance, an electric company may understand they are being targeted by hacking groups associated with a certain nation-state. Understanding the capabilities of that group—and how well those capabilities apply to the software and hardware at the electric company—can provide an intuition of the level of threat for which they must be prepared. Once this understanding is obtained, a variety of metrics can be better understood in context.

2.3.1 Problems at All Levels

The nature of business in both industry and government calls for wide-ranging collaborations of organizations of all sizes. For example, the government relies on hundreds of small businesses working under Small Business Innovation Research contracts as well as the traditional large government contractors. In the end, these organizations all collaborate and share data, and they do so electronically. Savvy attackers will actively seek out the smaller organizations—the ones with the least protected enterprise networks. They leverage these systems as launching pads for larger attacks (as in the attacks against South Korea in 2009, [17]) or an ingress points to larger organizations (as in the Target breach of 2014, [59]). Standards—whether from government or industry—are needed to increase security of our Internet as a whole. However, such standards cannot be static based on a current picture of the adversary; they must be forward-leaning and capture the essence of the ever-evolving nature of cyber threat actors.

2.3.2 Realizing Proactive Cyber Threat Intelligence

In order to realize the upper layers of the cyber threat intelligence model we outline in this chapter, there needs to be a change in mindset on cybersecurity—especially for corporations beyond the Fortune 100. In our research, we regularly talk with cyber threat intelligence practitioners across a variety of industries and (anecdotally) have found that large financial and technology companies—who are often considered the forefront of security—have a very different mindset for cyber threat intelligence. They are already embracing intelligence beyond situational awareness. The personnel in these offices often have military experience and understand the nuance of communicating the value of what they do to management, despite its inherent complexity. However, moving beyond these more exclusive sectors the story changes; the intelligence focus is primarily on situational awareness. The general lack of corporate investment in cyber threat intelligence beyond situational awareness necessitates a shift in culture and priorities. Leaders at every successful company understand their competitors in the marketplace—and have a plan of how to either best them or differentiate from them. However, the leaders of most companies do not understand their would-be cyber-attackers—despite the amount of damage they can cause to a firm. The problem is that for a corporation with a lower market cap, prioritizing cyber threat intelligence with an ambiguous value proposition is a difficult case to make. There are several possible and complementary ways to address this. One way is through establishing standards for threat intelligence within a corporation. Government standards—perhaps as a prerequisite to receiving shared information—and standards imposed by insurance companies are two obvious mechanisms. These can provide more near-term value to additional threat intelligence personnel. A second way is through executive-level education. A more informed C-suite and board will lead to more sound decisions on dealing with the cyber adversary. Ultimately, showing value and increasing education will lead to better investment in the right type of threat intelligence. Perhaps we can tip the scales back in favor of the defender and make "offense dominant" cybersecurity an anachronism.

This chapter highlighted the utility that cyber threat intelligence provides to an organization and how information about the ever-changing cyber threat landscape can help improve an organization's defensive posture. Additionally, some of the difficulties in realizing wide-scale cyber threat intelligence adoption were discussed and addressed. In the next chapter, we will discuss, in detail, the online hacker communities from which a lot of cyber threat intelligence is derived. By introducing the structure and layout of these hacker communities in the next chapter, we hope to familiarize the reader with ways in which these communities operate. Subsequently we will discuss the implementation of real cyber threat intelligence gathering systems, built on top of the data from these hacker communities, and covered in succeeding chapters.

3

Understanding Darkweb Malicious Hacker Forums

3.1 Introduction

For companies and institutions of all kinds, matters regarding the protection of Intellectual Property (IP) and Personally Identifiable Information (PII) from cyber-breaches and data-leaks are demanding higher financial investment. With the discovery of Stuxnet, offensive and defensive cyber-capabilities have become a tool in military arsenals worldwide and are on the cusp of shifting the global landscape of military power. With the expanding yield of cyber-related activities, understanding the actors creating, manipulating, and distributing malicious code becomes a paramount necessity.

After discussing the commercial importance of cyber threat intelligence in Chapter 2, we will begin learning how these cyber threat intelligence systems are built. The first logical step, which will be covered in this chapter, is to introduce the online hacker communities from which so much cyber threat intelligence derives. In this chapter, we report on the results of an exploration of black hat hacker forums on both the Internet and crypto-networks (in particular those accessed via the Tor-browser). We report on the structure, content, and standards of behavior within these forums. Throughout, we highlight how these communities augment the activities of the malicious hackers who participate.

Some of the English-language forums we will discuss are accessible though the Tor-network only, while the web forums addressing Russian speakers are most often found on the surface-layer Internet. These arenas of communication between malicious hackers allow insights into concerns, motivations, and goals as well as the environment in which they act. An intimate understanding of these communities will greatly aid proactive cybersecurity [9], by allowing cybersecurity practitioners to better understand their adversaries. While the structure of these forums largely resembles similar platforms, it is in the content and members that they differ.

Valuable insight into the structure and culture of hacker communities can be gained by focusing on forums where hacking techniques and exploits are created, shared [104], and distributed [23, 41]. Furthermore, these platforms often enforce rules of conduct, discuss the legitimacy of future endeavors, and negotiate targets [51, 9]. As such, forums constitute arenas in which the propagation of hacking techniques as well as discussion on cracking and ethics take place [41, 25]. Concerns, ambitions, and modi operandi of malicious hackers are showcased in forums, suggesting that a profound understanding of these communities will aid in early detection of cyber-attacks. The study in this chapter represents initial research in this direction.

The remainder of this chapter is organized as follows. In Section 3.2 we present background material. We then review our exploration methodology in Section 3.3. Structure and content of these online community areas are described in Sections 3.4 and 3.5, respectively. Finally, we conclude in Section 3.6.

3.2 Background

Many of the individuals behind cyber-operations—outside of government-run labs or military commands—rely on a significant community of hackers, preferably interacting through a variety of online forums (as means to both stay anonymous and to reach geographically dispersed collaborators). The distribution of *MegalodonHTTP* Remote Access Trojan (RAT) utilized the amateur black hat platform, HackForum. Five people accused of the malware's creation or distribution resided in three European countries requiring law enforcement to cooperate internationally in pursuit of the malicious hackers' arrest [55]. The international nature of the cyber-domain—the organization of cooperating malicious hackers as well as their international targets—transcends not only territorial executive powers, but adds to the importance of virtual communication platforms. Oftentimes—as in the case with *LulzSec* [95] and *Megalodon-HTTP*—the hackers are highly unlikely to ever meet each other in person. As we will describe later in Section 3.5, malicious hackers frequently suggest that providing any personally identifiable information is regarded as unsafe practice. This might hint at the benefits that online communities and other anonymizing services provide for netizens who want their physical existence to remain hidden and separate from their online persona and activities.

3.2.1 Darknet and Clearnet Sites

"The Onion Router" (Tor) is free software dedicated to protect the privacy of its users by obscuring traffic analysis as a form of network surveillance [30]. After downloading and installing the small software package, the Tor browser may be started like any other application. The network traffic is guided through a number of volunteer-operated servers (also called "nodes") rather than making a direct connection. Each node of the network encrypts the information which it blindly passes on, neither registering where the traffic came from nor where it is headed [30], disallowing any tracking. Each session of surfing the Internet through Tor utilizes different pathways through virtual tunnels. Tor further allows publishing websites without ever disclosing the location of the hosting server. Addresses to websites hosted on this hidden service use the ".onion" extension and do not render outside the Tor-network. Effectively, this allows not only for anonymized browsing (the IP-address revealed will only be that of the exit node), but also for circumvention of censorship.[1] For journalists, activists, and individuals living under repressive regimes, Tor allows a private and safe manner to communicate. Here we will refer to "darkweb" as synonymous with the anonymous communication services crypto-networks like the ones that Tor provide and which stand in contrast to "deepweb" which commonly refers to websites hosted on the open portion of the Internet (the "clearnet"), but not indexed by search engines [60]. Corporate websites supporting employees and library catalogs are good examples for deepweb presences. Additionally, dynamic websites which display content according to user requirements are also difficult to index [108]. Websites hosted on crypto-networks like Tor, such as Freenet, I2P, Hyperboria Network, M-Web, Shadow Web, and others are collectively referred to as "darkweb." Although the "darknet" describes a less populous, less expansive antecedent of the "darkweb," it is the term most commonly found in use by the people who frequent it. In contrast, "clearnet" is a term employed by Tor-users pointedly exposing the lack of anonymity provided by the surface-layer Internet [60].

3.2.2 Malicious Hacking

The hacker subculture has been the subject of many publications, amongst them Steven Levy's seminal "hackers" [63], which outlines ideological premises that many early computer geeks and programmers shared. The machines comprising the early computers were extensions of the self [111], which might compliment the creative ownership and the demand for free software that permeated Levy's account [63]. The term "hacker" in recent use (and especially in popular media) has become restricted to individuals who seek unauthorized

---

[1] See the Tor Project's official website (https://www.torproject.org/) and Tor's "About"-page (https://www.torproject.org/about/overview.html.en) for more details

access to computers and computer networks not their own with the purpose of manipulating, stealing, logging or altering data or structures [40, 104]. In this limitation the term becomes synonymous with "crackers"—a label more befitting those who indeed appear to solely pursue destruction and havoc. These are the activities more likely to be linked to criminal activities [46]. The term "crackers" itself derives from the practice of cracking passwords or levels in online and video games. Likewise, black hat hackers (or "black hats") employ their sometimes significant skills and knowledge toward illicit goals (e.g., financial fraud and identity theft). However, the hacker community is much more diverse. From meticulous tinkerers, phreakers [63], technology-savvy libertarians [25], and ideology-driven script kiddies or "vandals," as Jaishankar [46] calls hacktivists [109], "hacker" signifies everybody who uses his or her computer in innovative and creative ways [63]. Yet the hacker population encompasses divergent skill levels, motivations, and purposes as well as various modi operandi. New to programming and computer technology, "n00bs" or "newbies" stand at the beginning of their could-be hacking career. Script Kiddies (also called "Skiddies" or "Skids") utilize programs (scripts, tools, kits, etc.) created by more highly skilled crafters [40], whereas highly knowledgeable and experienced hackers see themselves as part of an elite ("leet") or, in hacker argot, replacing letters with numerals, "1337" [40].

3.2.3 Online Communities

The focus on web-forums so far was limited to forums on the clearnet [43, 1, 9, 60, 68, 92] and more often on a diversity of social media outlets in respect to activism and social organization as well as online games [52, 85, 44, 15, 49]. Many aspects of Internet forums have been the subject of academic research, for example in regard to their usability in social science or psychology research [41, 101] or as a form of technologically enabled communication amongst individuals [111, 7]. In the field of Social and Cultural Anthropology, an entirely new field, "Netnography" [58, 101, 24], is dedicated to conducting research in various online settings on diverse Internet-communities.

Hackers of all skills and motivations experience scholarly scrutiny focusing on manifold aspects [25, 63, 51]. The emergence of cyber-activism [31, 72], culminating in the heyday of Anonymous and associated hacktivists, earned not only headlines but also scholarly attention [105, 95]. Malicious hackers are the subject particularly of criminological studies [113, 39, 23, 41, 43, 40, 42, 110, 45, 68]. While scholars of diverse social sciences have gained insights into online behavior, the "darkweb" so far has elicited a lot less attention than the "clearnet." Beyond a technical introduction to the "darkweb" [16], Hsinchun Chen's group examines terrorism as portrayed on suspected jihadi-websites [21]. There are also studies on black hat-forums hosted on the "darkweb," which focus on trust in the anonymized environment of crypto-networks [60] and which concentrate on the social relationships in the presence of mutual distrust [77].

3.3 Methodology and Scope

Tor-hosted platforms are often shorter lived than their clearnet counterparts: sites migrate frequently or alternate through multiple addresses and their availability (uptime) is unreliable. Through search engines and spider services on the Tor-network, we were able to find more than 100 forums populated by malicious hackers. Other platforms were discovered through links posted on forums either on the Tor-network or on the clearnet. Most of these forums use English to communicate (70), but French (8), Russian (18), Swedish (2), and various other languages (5) are also used. On the clearnet, we found more than 150 forums for malicious hackers, the majority of which are English-speaking (52), 34 are in Russian, 40 in Arabic, 7 each in Farsi, Vietnamese and Mandarin. To gain access, most require registration and agreement to forum-rules. Registration and log-in often include completing CAPTCHA verification codes or images, solving puzzles, and answering questions to prevent automated entry and DDoS-attacks, thus requiring manual action.

Our initial nonparticipant observation [101] in different forums hosted in various languages had the purpose of exploring community structures, the interactions, and communication amongst the members of these platforms as well as the contents. Nonparticipant or minimal participant observation on these forums extends up to more than one year at the time of writing and is ongoing. While the structural organization of forums into boards, child boards, threads, and posts therein may mostly resemble more familiar platforms, the content differs significantly. The technical environment, social interaction, and predominant topics become especially interesting with malicious hackers. The members—at least to some degree—are profoundly familiar with the very same technology that constitutes the boundaries and limitations of their environment. They have the skills to negotiate and manipulate their technical surroundings should they wish to do so. All observed forums thus require agreement to a set of rules as part of the registration process. darkweb-hosted marketplaces, which are distinct from forums in that they are designed specifically for exchanging of

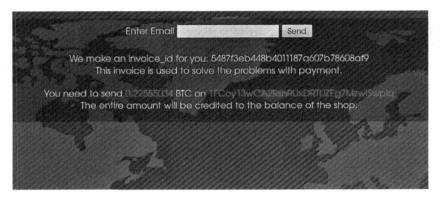

Figure 3.1.   Screenshot from a (paid) invite-only English-language Tor-hosted malicious hacker forum, taken December 2015. The BTC-amount indicated exchanges for USD100.

illicit goods and services, are repeatedly hacked to test them for their security and anonymity. Yet, the majority of the forum-populations appear to follow the forum-usage rules for their community. Perhaps this is due to the requirement to accept the forum-regulations during the registration-process that is absent in most marketplaces. Perhaps forums also constitute community through interaction with like-minded others more than trading on marketplaces. Nonetheless, discussions arise frequently on how to improve the forum experience. Many forums feature different access levels, granting more information and activity options to vetted members. For our research, we conducted observations in forums that required registration, but were otherwise unrestricted. Other platforms grant access only with invitation code, after payment or after a formal application, questionnaire, and online-interview (Figure 3.1).

3.4 Forum Structure and Community Social Organization

The structure of online forums entails two aspects: the structure of the technical environment as well as the social structure (and dynamics) organizing the community. Online-forums constitute technical environments with potentially malleable restraints. These user-oriented platforms have the sole purpose of enabling communication while providing the opportunity for the emergence of a community of like-minded individuals—regardless of their geophysical location.

3.4.1 Technical Structure

Administrators set up darkweb-forums with communication safety in mind. During registration (though not necessarily with every log-in) every prospective member has to complete CAPTCHAS, answer simple questions, solve puzzles, or complete simple arithmetic operations after agreeing to a specific set of rules.

Further safety measures are member-specific and member-supplied data such as email, PIN-number or mnemonics and often the member's public PGP-key.[2] Another precaution the individual user is urged to take is the employment of *Tails* (The Amnesiac Incognito Live System). This free operating system (based on Debian GNU/Linux) is run from a CD or USB stick and wipes the RAM once the computer shuts down[3]—leaving no trace of the past session. Tails is portable so that it can be used even on a public or shared-use computer. The pre-installed browser is thought to intensify the level of privacy when browsing the Tor- or I2P-network.

It is further recommended that the person at the keyboard disable JavaScript via a button in the browser. Not only is JavaScript known as being particularly vulnerable to software exploits [5], but it is also considered to be a weak spot which can easily be used to track and identify Tor-users. A technique dubbed (device-) "fingerprinting" is employed by third parties to track Internet users. JavaScript is one of the variety of characteristics that informs on the type of browser used as well as screen properties [88, 3]. Many darkweb-hosts therefore avoid JavaScript, which is a practice that appears to be widely regarded as enhancing security and also seems to improve the reputation of the respective forum. In another attempt to add security measures and gain members' trust, some forums' administrators will avoid time-stamping posts.

While forums need to feature techniques and mechanisms to enhance anonymity and privacy to gain support, it appears that strategies users employ to protect themselves are mainly limited to disguising the traces they leave on the darkweb. In order to diffuse the online persona, an individual could establish different monikers, with alternating interests (as indicated by browsing habits), use fake (written) accents, and register a multitude of anonymous email accounts. Irregular Tor-usage and connecting through ever-changing routing locations and Tor-bridges help defy tracking attempts and pattern-detection. A safe darkweb-second life therefore needs to become a puzzle with pieces being

---

[2] In English-language forums typically PGP-encryption is encouraged, online communities hosted in other languages (e.g. French and Italian) occasionally suggest the use of GPG (GNU Privacy Guard).

[3] Tails only uses RAM storage space, which is automatically erased after the computer shuts down.

widely dispersed, thus rendering the puzzle unsolvable. However, such a focus on security makes participation in an online community nearly impossible, as we will see later in Section 3.4.5.

3.4.2 The Process of Forum Registration

The means and tools of communication in the observed forums are public threads or private messages ("pm"). Plug-ins for instant chat platforms like Jabber and ICQ are sometimes provided and are gateways to platforms beyond.[4] The first step in the registration process consists of the agreement to official forum rules.[5] Most often that means to abstain from posting child pornography and to refrain from expressing any form of discrimination and racism. Trolls—provocative virtual trouble seekers who seemingly enjoy replying to other members' posts in a mere slanderous manner—are also not welcome. Moreover, the registration process focuses on the essentials of what the user might need (username, password) as well as on safety. During registration the prospective user may decide whether to receive emails from other users and the administrators. The chosen username then becomes the handle by which the user will be recognized by other members of the forum and which can be enhanced graphically. Other forms of personalization are signature block-like short statements that are printed at the bottom of each of the user's posts. It can be suggested that online handle and signature block serve to add a character dimension to the virtual persona.

3.4.3 Forums' Boards and Their Content

Good *OpSec*,[6] which is often stressed on darkweb forums' *Introduction* general information board and tutorials, recommends the employment of different usernames on each and every website, though to maintain reputation across sites, users may ignore this recommendation. All of a user's online handles, passwords and posts—the online personas—should be as different from the real world individual as possible. Members find buttons to their account, private messages, and to log off in the header of the page. Within the account, settings like email-address, password and other customization tools are found (depending on the forum).

---

[4] While Jabber allows members to contact each other independently of the forum, ICQ provide (private) chat-rooms and access to groups not associated with the forum.
[5] The broadcasting of rules also helps to describe the scope of the forum.
[6] "Operation Security" refers to the protection of personal identifiable information recommended for everyone on the darkweb.

Discussion forums addressing English-speakers on the darkweb consist of boards and sub-boards (also called "child-boards") filled with threads concerned with different topics. An "introduction" board is commonly heading the page, on which new members are encouraged to present themselves. A *General Discussion*-board hosts threads of importance to every member, for example "forum news," "news" (mainstream media), "privacy," and "safety." The English-speaking forums typically feature boards concerned with carding (financial fraud), hacking, cybersecurity, dumps or leaks (release of hacked data), and sometimes doxing (release of personal information). A few of these platforms also share malware code. Members of the forums can either start discussions, that is, new threads, in any of these boards or post comments on existing ones. The newest threads will most often appear at the top of the list of discussions within a (child-)board. The same is true for the replies within individual threads.

While the structural environment of Russian hacker forums remain similar to their English counterparts 3.2, there are several marked differences that are worth noting. The most striking difference lies in the amount of Russian forums hosted on the clearnet. Whether Russian hackers are less worried about *OpSec* and possible legal repercussions, or if they simply prefer the more stable environment that the clearnet offers,[7] we do not yet know. A limited availability of bandwidth might be a technological barrier to using Tor. Furthermore, in some countries the website of the Tor-project is blocked and inaccessible to the general public. Still, the majority of Russian clearnet-forums closely resemble the darkweb-forums in their general structure, with features such as invite-only access, CAPTCHA, and heavy monitoring by administrators enforcing forum rules. In Figure 3.2, the structural organization of an exemplary Russian black-hat forum, which does not generally differ from its English counterparts, is shown. The page breakdown is as follows:

1 Темы ("Themes"). Shows the number of original posts for each thread topic.
2 Сообщений ("Messages"). Shows the total number of messages for each thread topic.
3 Последнее сообщение ("Last Messages"). Shows the title of the last thread, its date, and the user that posted it.

---

[7] The availability of Tor-hosted websites ("uptime") is much less reliable than those hosted on the surface-layer Internet. Due to the tunneling through multiple nodes, the loading of Tor-hosted sites also takes longer than direct connections. To evade monitoring many administrators migrate between a number of web-addresses, though that practice is more common with darkweb-marketplaces.

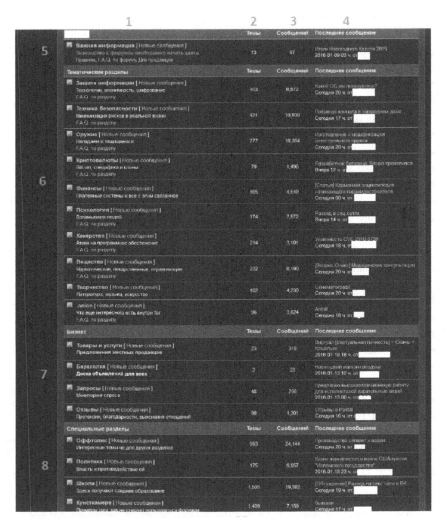

Figure 3.2. Screenshot from a Russian-language clearnet-forum, taken January 2016.

4 Важная информация ("Important Information"). This category contains
  important information about the forum, and new users are encouraged to read
  this first.
5 Тематические разделы ("Thematic Sections"). Contains a list of thread topics including: Protection of Information, Technical Safety, Weapons, Cryp-
  tocurrency, Finances, Psychology, Hacking, Substances (illegal as well as

prescription drugs), Creation (literature, music, art), .onion (link-list of other Tor-hosted websites).

6 Бизнес ("Business"). This category or section contains all of the topics related to the sale of products or services. Topics include: Wares and Services, Flea Market (a public board for all to use), Requests (for among others hacking services), Reviews (of forum-/marketplace-vendors).

7 Специальные разделы ("Special Sections"). Contains a list of topics not related to the aforementioned, including: "Off Topic,"[8] "Politics," "School" (tests, exams, cheating – hinting at the presumed age of some members), and finally "Curiosities."

3.4.4 The Social Structure of Malicious Hacker-Forums

In addition to the graphical structure and forum-contents, social hierarchies can be readily observed. Like clearnet-forums, the social organization of all of the observed darkweb-hosted malicious hacker-forums feature a multilayered social structure with status-respective tasks [1]. The vetting process itself differs between forums, but it generally entails frequent participation and showcasing of skills. The former is frequently emphasized and the accounts of insufficiently active members may be suspended. This requirement may suggest that much effort is dedicated to community-building as nonsociability is punished. It also serves toward the goal of preventing lurking, which appears to be regarded as suspicious behavior. Showcasing of skills—while currently not a ubiquitous demand—generally suggests to serve multiple purposes: for the forum it serves in identifying skillful members and aids in building up resources to be shared within the community. Both of these characteristics vet a platform to attract more skillful members and notoriety. For the providing individual, code samples and successful endeavors not only links them with like-minded collaborators, but also aid in improving their social status and ranking within the community.

Every forum needs a person to create this virtual gathering space in the first place, as well as keep it online and maintain the user database. Therefore, as creator and host, administrators ("admin(s)") are found heading the social hierarchy in every forum. The site administrators have the power to admit new members, delete accounts, and change the structural development as well as the scope of the forum. Administrators decide whether or not to institute a structure of layered access to and within the forum by setting or removing hurdles

---

[8] "Off Topic"-sections are often spaces provided to both answer the apparent need of members to sometimes discuss topics unrelated to the forum's general theme as well as to maintain the integrity of the other hosted boards

like invite-only or set minimum access-requirements to certain boards. Residing on the next lower-level, moderators (or short "mods") are often responsible for specific boards and specialize in specific topics. The subject-matter experts censor the contributions of members by selecting and either moving or deleting off-topic posts and thus play a crucial role in enforcing forum-rules. In forums where assets [92] such as tutorials and malware are provided, moderators also filter and vet community resources. The quality control of resources includes ensuring the functionality and nature of code. Scripts that are found to be potentially malicious for forum-members are usually not hosted on the forum. Ratings from fellow forum-members paired with activity level and seniority (i.e., duration of membership) create a system of rank within the general forum population. As noted for hackers elsewhere [51, 41], online communities follow the principle of meritocracy and base a hacker's reputation and social status on his/her skills and accomplishments. The peer-rankings constitute the social status of an online persona. The higher the ratings of a member the more trust is allotted to any kind of contribution they submit. The accuracy of provided information and the usefulness, functionality, and efficacy of code are crucial for positive ratings. Oftentimes high peer-ratings will grant access to hidden boards and the member may apply to becoming a moderator in response to future "job" announcements. Generally, expertise is elemental to become a moderator; however, other moderators seem to be selected based on their popularity. A positive reputation is of great value beyond the forum in question. Newly established, highly specified platforms are set up to allow for a smaller community with purpose. Members are usually hand-picked from existing, more general forums. At the bottom of a forum's social spectrum, "newbies" (or "noobs") are often restricted to their own boards and are expected to learn and get vetted before advancing to boards with more advanced topics.

They are often aggressively reprimanded should they decide to post questions deemed as inadequate for threads of more highly skilled hackers. Social mobility lies for many forum-participants in the sharing of knowledge or in the showcasing of expertise. The structure and organization of hacker communities demand the semiprivate publication of hacks. If a member wants to advance within the community, s/he has to showcase her/his endeavors and thus risks unsolicited attention from the cybersecurity industry and law enforcement.

3.4.5 The Double-Edged Sword of the Hacker Meritocracy

Since social status is gained through proofs of expertise [51, 41], but uploading evidence of malicious activity puts malicious hackers at risk of attracting the attention of law enforcement, malicious hackers vying for social status face

Figure 3.3.   Screenshot from an English-language Tor-hosted malicious hacker-forum, taken July 2015.

a dilemma, and mediums allowing the concealment of personally identifiable information are therefore important. Negotiating the precious balance between notoriety and possible legal repercussions is aggravated by the use of monikers as near single markers of recognition. PGP-keys also frequently serve—aside from their purpose as guarantors of privacy—as proof of authenticity in online communication, but as such are invariably tied to the moniker. Therefore, as mentioned before, malicious hackers who use identical handles across multiple platforms as a way to "carry" their reputation with them are at an elevated risk of being tracked by law enforcement. Should they be identified on one platform all their activities can easily be traced across the networks. On the other hand, advantages of being recognized include instant access to arenas closed to "nobodies." For vendors, standing in high regard translates directly into profits.

Establishing a reputation is time-intensive and laborious, perhaps even more so in an environment that is as discouraging of trust as the Internet. The mechanisms of establishing good standing within the online community of hackers relies on the number of posts and their relevance. Members showcasing high levels of activity on the forum and expertise will improve their status fastest. Contributors rate each others posts according to content and perceived attitude. The rank earned is publicly displayed, as seen in Figure 3.3, alongside the moniker. Seniority indicates a member's loyalty to the forum and might encourage the administrator to offer moderator positions. Occasionally, different levels of access are granted to vetted members (Section 3.7). Under these circumstances, the desire of popular *darknetizens* to transfer earned reputation across different platforms becomes conceivable. Accordingly, we observed highly regarded malicious hackers and carders use the same moniker in multiple forums and social media sites.

Considering that PGP-keys frequently serve as proof of identity, this practice appears to be an audacious *OpSec*-fault. For example, the developer of the Phoenix exploit kit—a software toolkit designed to compromise various pieces of common software—went by the moniker of "AlexUdakov" across several forums [115], one of which was the seized crime-forum "Darkode" [54, 81]. Russian forum members will often refer to other forums and marketplaces where they have sold hacking products, or where they have an established profile. This aids in the discovery of new forums and marketplaces, but does not lend itself to protecting the anonymity of the user. In this way it would be easy to trace members, regardless of their handle across multiple forums, across marketplaces and forums through their advertised pieces of software or malware. Similarly, both clearnet- and Tor-hosted Russian-language forums utilize some form of member ranking system, whereby users may elevate their status on a forum by making a certain number of posts, providing especially valuable knowledge or even samples of free malware.

3.4.6 The Russian Forum-cum-Marketplaces

One of the most fascinating aspects of Russian hacker and carder forums is the use of Internet slang "Padonkaffsky Jargon" or "Olbanian" that permeates every aspect of the darkweb, deepnet, and clearnet alike. Russian forums also differ from their English counterparts in that many forums also act as marketplaces. It is crucial to take the social and legal landscape of Russia into account to gain a better understanding of the inner workings of Russian forums, and the users that frequent them. The (relative) impunity for hacking-related offenses may explain the clearnet-hosting of many forums addressing Russian-speakers. Although Russia does have laws that govern cybercrime, they generally fail to reach prosecution unless offenses are committed inside the Russian Federation. A further complicating factor is the fact that the US and Russia have no extradition treaty—a circumstance that is effectively creating a safe haven for (malicious) hackers. Coupled with the over-educated and underemployed population, we find a breeding ground for malicious hackers seeking to earn a living with their technical skills. Evidence of this can be seen in 17-year-old hacker Sergey Taraspov, from St. Petersburg. Mr. Taraspov, along with a small team of hackers, allegedly wrote a piece of malware that targeted point-of-sale (POS) software, and sold it for USD2,000 (about two months' salary for a programmer) on a Russian forum/marketplace. This malware was, in turn, used by around forty individuals to steal over 110 million American credit card numbers in the "Target"-data breach of 2013 [83]. This is one example of the more notorious uses of Russian malware to exploit American companies, but attacks like these happen on a daily basis. It is not the intent of this chapter to exhaustively discuss the legal landscape for hackers in Russia, but it is worth noting some of the idiosyncrasies.

We have observed that Russian forums vary greatly in exclusivity. Some are very easy to gain access into, or even allow guests to peruse the forum topics. Others allow the creation of a forum-account by simply signing up and providing an email address. The exclusive Russian forums, on both the darkweb and clearnet, are much more suspicious of prospective users and use certain countermeasures against unwanted entry. Many require a code that can only be obtained by forum admins or other vetted users. Some require that a prospective user submit a sample of their code or malware as part of the vetting process. Several forums will even fluctuate between open and closed registration, presumably to keep up with user registration and to thwart unwanted access. As one would expect, these exclusive forums are home to highly skilled hackers. As seen in Figure 3.4, and its translation into English, the administrators believe their forum to be suitable only for true professionals, and advise less sophisticated users to seek alternative places to gain knowledge. These forums, which are easy to gain access to, are teeming with script kiddies. It is possible to discuss or even purchase many different types of malware on these less-exclusive forums, but the products might at times be outdated. Apparently, much less effort is extended toward uncluttering these lower-tier marketplace-forums, making noteworthy and valuable products harder to reach. The more exclusive the forum is, the greater the chance that it will provide newer, high-quality malware and exploit kits. Access to exclusive forums must be carefully obtained and can often be a lengthy process. Forum administrators will conduct online-interviews through private messages, either utilizing the exchange of PGP keys for identification purposes or through messaging protocols like Jabber or ICQ. It is the job of the administrators to keep forum-members safe from the prying eyes of law enforcement, researchers, and inactive lurkers. They take pride in spotting different types of prospective members. Russian hackers behave and even write in a certain way, identifying themselves as hackers, and obfuscating their communication—as well as their code.

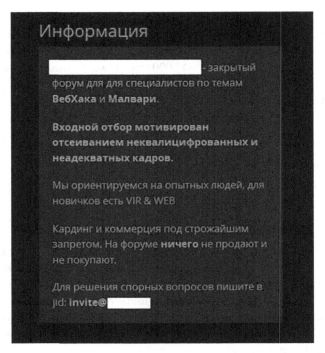

Figure 3.4.   Screenshot of "Welcome"-page of a closed Russian-language forum, taken December 2015.

The forum depicted in Figure 3.4 is closed to all "nonspecialists." The direct translation is as follows: "Information. This is a closed forum for specialists on the themes of hacking and malware. This discrimination is motivated [to deter] inadequate and unqualified people [trying to gain access]. We are focused on individuals with experience. For beginners there are other places like *VIR* and *WEB* [both links to forums known to be populated by script-kiddies]. Carding and commerce is strictly forbidden. On this forum nothing is sold or purchased. To resolve contentious issues, please write to JId [Jabber id]." As also observed in English forums, highly skilled malicious hackers sometimes appear to prefer a community of similarly sophisticated individuals and consequently discriminate against "newbies."

3.5 The Content of Observed Forums

While structure and organization of darkweb-hosted forums might be very similar to more familiar web-forums, the topics and concerns of the users vary distinctly. In the English clandestine darkweb people interested in cats, steampunk, and the latest conspiracy theories convene, but an abundance of arenas dedicated to child pornography (CP), drugs, and weapons can also be found. Other forums appear to be venues for sharing erotic images—whether involving real persons or cartoon characters. Trading places are also very popular among *darknetizens* and in many forums, marketplaces are discussed, including lengthy threads that seek information on the reliability of individual vendors and marketplaces in general. Links to other darkweb-sites and information on potentially fraudulent Web sites are especially useful in the absence of pervasive search engines and can be found on many forums. Forums addressing malicious hackers feature discussions on programming, hacking, and cybersecurity. Threads are dedicated to security concerns like privacy and online-safety—topics which plug back into and determine the structures and usage of the platforms.

3.5.1 The Common Boards

Oftentimes, the *Introduction*-board is dedicated to explaining the functions, extensions and buttons of the forum. Beyond technical advice, proper manners as well as measures of *OpSec* are discussed. The latter includes tips on staying anonymous and safe on the darkweb in general, which is a near ubiquitous topic on forums populated by malicious hackers. Threads concerned with the protection of members' anonymity are often pinned to the top of the list of threads within a (child-)board ("sticky threads"). Members are expected to adhere to manners, including to abstain from "trolling" (derisive posts for the mere purpose of provoking angry responses) and from posting prohibited material (most often child pornography). On many forums, "spamming" (posts of no informative value) and "grave-digging" (reviving of posts long abandoned) are considered ill-mannered. *General Discussion*-boards often feature news from the administrators, suggestions for the improvement of the forum, membership policies, information on the recruitment of moderators, and a relay of mainstream-news (especially in connection with news concerning the community). The sentencing of Ross Ulbricht, a.k.a. *Dread Pirate Roberts* (DPR), to life in prison for pioneering the concept of darkweb-supermarkets (DNMs) as the creator and administrator of the original Silkroad-Market (SR1) reverberated heavily on *General Discussion*-boards around the darkweb. However, this is also the place to deliberate about new movies, software as well as other products and popular items. In some cases, new members are required to contribute a set number of posts before being granted access to other parts of the forum. This board is also the place where answers to frequently asked questions (FAQs) are found.

3.5.2 The Flavored Boards

Hereafter, the titles of boards and their content strongly varies between forums according to their general theme. Forums addressing malicious hackers afford space for boards offering tutorials and guides for both novice and experienced malicious hackers as well as carders. In many forums, old malicious code is shared for practice purposes, which conforms to the hacker-ideal of self-education [51]. Members challenge each other by posting claims of their accomplishments, sometimes publishing either code or links to "dumps" (repositories, pastebins, or other data-sharing sites) containing hacked data. General information and discussions on software, malware, exploits, and vulnerabilities are ubiquitous. Discussions relating to hacking certain systems, advertisements for services, and the bartering of stolen data are also commonly encountered. Posters inquire about how to crack specific applications or they are seemingly working on a particular project and seek help (often eliciting responses). Though expressly prohibited by many forums, others do feature boards for doxxing—where personally identifiable and private information is shared for the purpose of harassing the exposed individuals (and their families and friends) in the real (physical) world. Comparatively harmless forms thereof typically include endless prank phone calls and the delivery of unordered food, but can be taken to extremes with events involving physical attacks and surprise visits by teams of law enforcement officers in response to supposed hostage crisis (also called "swatting") [86]. On almost all Russian forums, we observed rampant requests for hacking as a service (HaaS) (Section 3.5). For a reasonable amount of digital currency, a professional hacker offers a variety of tasks—from hacking a friend's email- or Facebook-account, to shutting down an entire website (DDoS). In yet another way, hacking is being democratized, the sale or provision of complete malicious code on forums being one such indication. But other than with malware, where minimal modification to target-specific needs still demands some basic skills, hiring a hacker does not require a basic understanding of coding, hacking, or malware. Merely investing thirty minutes on general research and installing the Tor-browser, newbies effectively become cyber threats. For many Russians (and citizens of the former Soviet Block), this is a way to earn an income. Whether they built the malware tool or just purchased it as an investment, they are able to turn around and use it to make money.

The post shown in Figure 3.5 is a hacker listing services for sale (HaaS). The sections include:

1 Topic title – Взлом почты и социальных сетей. Дешево, Взлом ("Hacking of Email and Social Media Accounts. Cheap, Hacking").

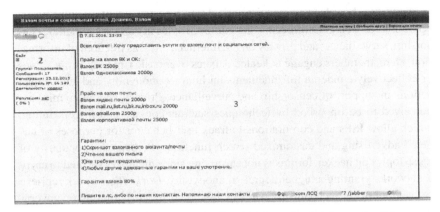

Figure 3.5. Screenshot of post in Russian forum/marketplace advertising Hacking-as-a-Service (HaaS), taken January 2016.

2 Forum user information, including his or her forum rating, number of posts written, date of post, user number, post classification, and reputation information.

3 Post – Translation:

Hi All! I want to provide hacking services for email and social media. Price for hacking VK and OK:
Hacking VK 2500 rubles
Hacking Classmates (similar to VK) 2000 rubles

Price for hacking email:
Hacking Yandex email 2000 rubles
Hacking mail.ru, list.ru, bk.ru, inbox.ru 2000 rubles
Hacking gmail.com 2500 rubles
Hacking corporate email 2500 rubles

Guarantee:
1) Screenshot of the hacking of the account/email
2) Reading your letter
3) We don't require payment in advance
4) Any other adequate safeguards at your discretion

Guarantee of hacking 80%

Send a private message or to one of the following contacts: (ICQ/Jabber/email)

Additional boards dedicated to political topics betray potential future cyber-operations as well as reinforce hacker culture. Topics in these areas include censorship, surveillance, and privacy on the Internet as well as freedom of information. Here, members engage in heated debates over basic rights and core values or collectively condemn infringements on Internet anonymity and authorities' actions in support of censorship and surveillance. Privacy and anonymity are perceived to be imperiled by techniques such as cookies and fingerprinting, which allow ISPs and corporations to track user behavior for purposes of targeted advertising and customized search functions. Perhaps the popularity of these topics on hacker-forums is not surprising since members vacated to cryptonetworks granting a higher degree of anonymity. *Darknetizens* seek reprieve from monitoring mechanisms whether instituted by corporations or government, even if they may not and do not plan to engage in illegal or unlawful activities.

3.5.3 Sentiments and Concerns

Many posts (not just in black hat forums) are laced with anticorporate and antigovernment sentiments or carry a negative connotation in regard to law enforcement and their efforts to stem unlawful activities on the darkweb. A member of an English-language darkweb-forum, for example, assured that "corporate media is an elitist-controlled brainwashing apparatus where truth is irrelevant" (observed December 2015). In fact, members and administrators of malicious hacker-forums are aware of the probable presence of law enforcement officers—right along with "nosy researchers and journalists" (observed September 2015). Suggestions to rid the forum of such unwanted guests include, but are not limited to, closing the forum off to new members and instituting invite-only access. Forcing members to contribute to the forum community sometimes exceeds a preset number of required posts per time frame and calls for tests of heart, such as proof of criminal activity or the fulfillment of a specific illegal task demanded by a moderator or administrator. However, the effectiveness of these measures in excluding law enforcement agents is a matter of discourse in the respective communities. Furthermore, not all members favor invite-only forums out of fear the topics and livelihood of the community might grow stale with a near static population. Though apparently in the minority, some appear to realize the futility of measures aiming at exclusivity and prefer to face the inevitable risks associated with their actions with good personal OpSec and a trust-no-one doctrine in order to evade criminal prosecution.

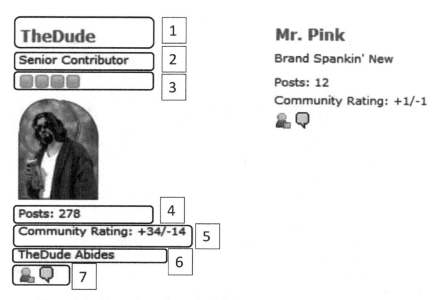

Figure 3.6. Screenshot of member-id thumbnails in an English-language darkweb-forum, taken January 2016. Key: (1) moniker; (2) community rank; (3) community rating summary; (4) number of posts; (5) positive/negative community ratings; (6) member quote; (7) contact.

In English-language forums, cultural references permeate platforms. Underdogs and antiheroes such as Edward Norton's nameless character in *Fight club*, Robert De Niro's character in *Taxi Driver*, Jeff Bridges' "The Dude" in *The Big Lebowski* (Figure 3.6) and "Verbal/Keyser Soze" from *The Usual Suspects* are well-liked profile pictures. Other recited pop-cultural icons are the "Cheshire Cat" of *Alice in Wonderland* and *Seinfeld*'s "Kramer." Images or short video replays of protagonists are displayed near online handles or citations appear in signature blocks. Monikers themselves sometimes are seen to hijack meaning in reference to these counterpopular characters. Many seem to be adopted because they find themselves standing apart from what normally busies the world (e.g., *Seinfeld*'s "Kramer" and "The Dude" (*The Big Lebowski*)). Seemingly weak and powerless they either emerge to be the lone survivors (e.g., "Verbal" in *The Usual Suspects*, "Mr. Pink" in *Reservoir Dogs*) (Figure 3.6) or escalate into outbursts of violence (e.g., the protagonist in *Taxi Driver*). Statements expressing political views or the author's perspective on society are often found in signature blocks, which are automatically displayed with every posting. Occasionally, links and invite-codes to alternate forums or marketplaces can also be found here.

3.5.4 Linguistic Characteristics

The self-identification of a hacker—whether malicious or not—is strongly reflected and transmitted through the use of a specific jargon ("leet"-speak). In English, specific letters can be replaced with numbers and characteristic abbreviations are used. All users of Russian forums express themselves in a sophisticated and popular Internet slang known as "Padonkaffsky Jargon" or "Olbanian." For example, Padonkaffsky Jargon utilizes many aspects of the Russian language, culture, and subculture. It entails a sophisticated system of alternate orthography. Alternate representations of vowels and consonant are based on word-pronunciation and not on standard-modern Russian orthography. In certain situations, such as in word-final position and when proceeding another devoiced consonant in a consonant-cluster, voiced consonants are pronounced and written in Internet slang like their devoiced counterparts. For example, the Russian "–В" (V), when in word-final position or preceding a consonant in some situations, is written as a "– Ф" (F). Similarly, Russian vowel reduction can also cause a change in orthography whereby an unstressed "– О" (O) is pronounced as an "– А" (A) and is represented as the latter in the context of the Internet. This sophisticated slang also implements a large amount of pop-culture references. As western pop-culture is well-liked in Russia and other countries of the former Soviet Union, references to it are represented in this write-only slang. Without expert knowledge of the Russian culture and language, it would be very difficult to parse out and understand forum discussions with any precision. On the Internet the written form is not only a formal representation of thought, but is the sole vehicle of communication.

3.5.5 Trading Places

Many Russian forums effectively act as marketplaces (Figure 3.7), where users can advertise and sell their wares. This is quite simply accomplished by setting up a board named "Commercial Area" or "For Sale" (as observed in January 2016). In this section of the forum, the first post of any thread will be written by the seller. His or her post will include a description of the item for sale, the price (in one of several digital currencies), and private contact information (Jabber, ICQ, or others) to invite conversation. The following posts are usually from prospective buyers asking questions, requesting demos, or even discrediting the seller and/or their products. With so many differing opinions, these discussions can get quite heated and even lead to users being banned. Many of these forum-marketplaces feature wallets to deposit digital currency into, but sometimes forum administrators serve as an escrow service. Products are most

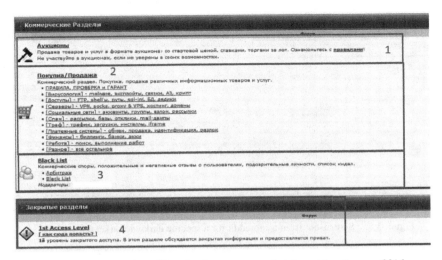

Figure 3.7. Screenshot of Russian forum-cum-marketplace, taken January 2016.

often verified before any funds are released to the seller. If a seller is misleading or fails to deliver the appropriate item, they are banned from the site. Similarly, buyers can be banned for not complying with the transaction rules. This is an effective way of enforcing forum norms in that it serves as deterrent for possible future transgressions (as we will show later, banned monikers are published on "Black Lists") while at the same time reinforcing the reliability of the forum as a trading place.

Figure 3.7 shows a section of a forum that also acts as a marketplace. The boards within the *Purchase/Sales* section are broken down as follows:

1 Аукционы ("Auctions")—On this board threads are constituted by items which are to be auctioned off (similar to Ebay).
2 Покупка/Продажа ("Buy/Sell")—This board contains different categories of items for sale. The list includes: (Market) "Rules"; "Verification and Guarantees"; "Virusology" (malware, exploits, networking, cryptology); "Access" (FTP, Shell, rooting, SQL-injection); "Servers" (VPN, socks, proxy & VPS, hosting, domains); "Social Media" (accounts, groups, hacking, and mailing); "Spam" (mailings, bases, responses, and dumps); "Traffic" (traffic, downloading, installs, iframe); "Payment Systems" (exchange, sale, indemnification, unlock); "Finance" (billing, banks, accounts); "Work" (search, execution of work).

Figure 3.8.   Screenshot from a subreddit for a specific darknet market (July 2016).

3 "Black list"—This board is dedicated to resolving commercial disputes, features positive and negative reviews about members, suspicious persons, and a list of banned usernames.
4 "Closed Forums"—This section contains all of the forums unavailable to insufficiently vetted users. The forum administrator presides over the admission into this section.

3.5.6 Subreddits

Reddit is a clearnet site that acts as a content aggregator where users can come together and form subcommunities focused on a specific topics. These subcommunities are called subreddits. Some subreddits, specifically the ones that are of interest to our research, are focused on the discussion of darknet exploit markets. Important information regarding the marketplace environment, including reviews of marketplaces, products, and vendors, are often discussed on these subreddits. These links and sentiments about markets can provide insight. For instance, we might learn to predict when popular opinion shifts with respect to a certain market. Subreddits also provide information concerning marketplaces and forums that are newly introduced or old ones that are shutting down. Figure 3.8 shows one such subreddit.

3.6 Conclusion

In this chapter, we took an in-depth look at the culture of black hat communities in web-forums. In particular, we were able to present the realization of social structure in an online environment, the mechanisms of social mobility, pop-cultural references, and linguistic characteristics. Social dynamics reinforce and maintain the communities and their structures. Forums are the arenas in which community norms are imposed, enforced, negotiated, and altered. Understanding the social organization not only improves our knowledge, but can also aid in preventing and tackling computer crime [39]. Because forums (and marketplaces) share resources such as malicious code and knowledge (how-to), they are driving the democratization of cyber-attacks. The devaluation of expertise allows for cyber-attacks to be carried out by actors with very few skills. A key information requirement that can be addressed by monitoring online forums is "which cyber-capabilities are available to an adversary?" The knowledge spread on these platforms through not only discussion, but provided by tutorials and free malware- and exploit kit-downloads allows for capabilities to spread quickly. New cyber tactics, identification of software vulnerabilities, and attack claims can spread rapidly in these environments. Additionally, the anonymity awarded to users of especially the darkweb enables hacktivists, cyber-mercenaries, military personnel in cyber-units, and those seeking to sell malware to evade legal restrictions such as export laws. Cyber-analysts must understand the culture of these communities and their topics of discourse in order to identify emerging cyber threats and capabilities. As we anticipate the relevance of hacking communities to only increase in the cyber domain, understanding these specialized online communities will become of critical importance for anticipating cyber threats, intelligence analysis, and understanding cyber capabilities available to adversaries who tap into the knowledge and resources of these communities.

In the next chapter, we will discuss techniques to gather data from these darknet communities and we will begin to illustrate how the mined information can provide valuable cyber threat intelligence. The performance of various data-mining and machine-learning techniques in the context of gathering cyber threat intelligence will also be discussed in the next chapter. This then lays the groundwork for later chapters (5 and 6) where we are able to start quantifying some aspects of these communities and markets.

4

Automatic Mining of Cyber Intelligence from the Darkweb

4.1 Introduction

Now that we have a better understanding of the hacker communities present on both the darknet and the clearnet, which were discussed in the previous chapter, we can begin to use data-mining and machine-learning techniques to aggregate and analyze the data from these communities, with a goal of providing valuable cyber threat intelligence. This chapter is an extension of the work in [80]. We present a system for cyber threat intelligence gathering, built on top of the data from communities similar to those presented in Chapter 3. At the time of writing, this system collects, on average, 305 high-quality cyber threat warnings each week. These threat warnings contain information regarding malware and exploits, many of which are newly developed and have not yet been deployed in a cyber-attack. This information can be particularly useful for cyber-defenders. Significantly augmented through the use of various data-mining and machine-learning techniques, this system is able to recall 92% of products in marketplaces and 80% of discussions on forums relating to malicious hacking, as labeled by a security analyst, with high precision. Additionally, we will present a model based on topic modeling used for automatic identification of new hacker forums and exploit marketplaces for data collection.

In succeeding sections, we will introduce a machine-learning-based scraping infrastructure to gather such intelligence from these online communities. We will also discuss the challenges associated with constructing such a system and how we addressed them. Figure 4.1 shows the number of detected threats for five weeks and Table 4.1 shows the database statistics at the time of writing, which indicates that only a small fraction of the data collected is hacking related. The vendor and user statistics cited only consider those individuals associated in the discussion or sale of malicious hacking-related material, as identified by the system.

Table 4.1. *Current database status*

Markets	Total number	27
	Total products	11991
	Hacking related	1573
	Vendors	434
Forums	Total number	21
	Topics/posts	23780/162872
	Hacking related	4423/31168
	Users	5491
Subreddits	Total number	33
	Topics/posts	3940/19601
	Hacking related	1654/8270

Specific contributions of this chapter include:

- Description of a system for cyber threat intelligence gathering from various social platforms from the Internet such as deepnet and darknet websites.
- The implementation and evaluation of learning models to separate relevant information from noise in the data collected from these online platforms.
- A machine-learning approach to aid security experts in the discovery of new relevant deepnet and darknet websites of interest using topic modeling—this reduces the time and cost associated with identifying new deepnet and darknet sites.

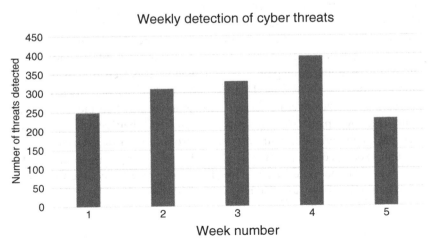

Figure 4.1. Weekly detection of cyber threats.

The chapter is organized as follows: in Section 4.2, we give a system overview describing our data collection system. We then describe the challenges encountered in storing the noisy, semistructured data from the web in a well-structured relational database using advanced data-mining techniques in Section 4.3. We also provide evaluation results demonstrating the performance of these models. Finally, related work is presented in Section 4.4.

4.2 System Overview

To find sites from which to collect data, security analysts used Tor-based search engines and spider services to aggregate a list of hacker forums and markets. Some clearnet forums also will share links that direct to darknet hacking forums and markets. Figure 4.2 gives the overview of the system, which consists of three main modules built independently before integration. The system is currently fully integrated and actively collecting cyber threat intelligence.

Crawler: The crawler is a program designed to traverse the website and retrieve HTML documents. Topic-based crawlers [75, 19] have been used for focused crawling where only webpages of interest are retrieved, versus traversing all webpages. More recently, focused crawling was employed to collect forum discussions from the darknet [37]. Due to structural differences and varying access control measures (CAPTCHAs, rate-limiting, etc.) in many markets and forums, we have designed unique crawlers for many different platforms. Our crawler implementations had to address technical challenges such as intermittent uptime from sites and duplicated links creating cycles to gather product information from markets and forum discussions threads.

Parser: The parser is used to extract well-structured information from the HTML pages of marketplaces (regarding sale of malware/exploits) and hacker forums (discussion regarding services and threats). This well-structured information is stored in a relational database. We maintain two databases, one for marketplaces and the other for forums. Similar to the crawlers, most platforms require their own parser, due to structural differences between the sites. The parser also communicates with the crawler from time to time for collection of temporal data, communicating a list of relevant webpages to the crawler to be re-crawled to get time-varying data. For markets we collect the following important product fields to be stored in the database:

- item_title
- item_description
- vendor_name

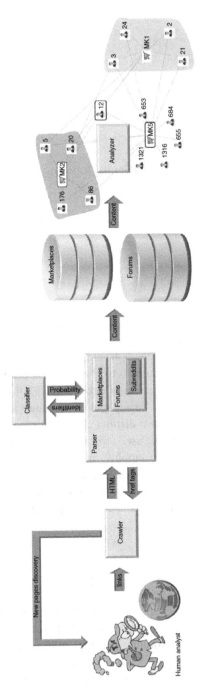

Figure 4.2. System overview.

- shipping_details
- item_reviews
- items_sold
- CVE
- items_left
- transaction_details
- ratings

For forums and subreddits we collect the following fields:

- topic_content
- post_content
- topic_author
- post_author
- author_status
- reputation
- topic_interest

Classifier: Automating the process of classifying a webpage as being relevant to the topic of interest greatly expedites data collection. As the crawler traverses darknet links, it is important that the classification portion of the pipeline is able to keep up. By requiring humans to classify sites, products, and threads as relevant or irrelevant (in the context of cybersecurity), there is a bottleneck in the classification stage and the throughput of the data-gathering pipeline is greatly diminished. We address two distinct classification challenges. First, to discover new relevant websites, we used topic modeling to determine if a given webpage is relevant. Second, we employ machine learning with an expert-labeled dataset to detect relevant products and topics from marketplaces and forums, respectively. These classifiers are integrated into the parser to filter out products and threads relating to drugs, weapons, etc. not relevant to malicious hacking.

4.3 Evaluation

Our first major classification challenge involves designing a model to determine if a given product, forum thread, or subreddit (subreddits are forums in which information relating to forums and marketplaces are discussed—this can be viewed as meta-content) discussion is relevant to malicious hacking. The second major classification challenge is to identify new, relevant marketplaces/forums; that is, looking at a given webpage, we wish to know whether this webpage is a page on a darknet marketplace or hacker forum. These problems are binary classification problems; the output is a 1 or 0, relevant or not-relevant. We look at both supervised and semi-supervised approaches to address the first classification problem and topic modeling for the second. We now provide an overview of the approaches used and then discuss some of the technical challenges associated with each classification problem.

4.3.1 Supervised Approaches

Supervised learning is a class of machine learning that is often, but not exclusively, used for classification problems. In supervised learning, a classification model is built with data that has ground-truth class labels (i.e., samples for which the true label is known). After the training period, the constructed model can be used to predict class labels for samples in which the ground-truth label is not known. In the context of this chapter, the classification challenge is to predict if a given darknet marketplace product or forum thread (sample) is hacking-related or not (class label). Our ground-truth dataset was constructed by providing a subset of the data to a security analyst to label as hacking-related or not.

Naive Bayes Classifier (NB). Naive Bayes is a probabilistic classifier which uses Bayes theorem with an independent attribute assumption. During training we compute the conditional probabilities of a sample of a given class having a certain attribute. We also compute the prior probabilities for each class, that is, the fraction of the training data belonging to each class. Naive Bayes assumes that the attributes are statistically independent; hence the likelihood for a sample S represented with a set of attributes a associated with a class c is given as, $\Pr(c|S) = P(c) \times \prod_{i=1}^{d} \Pr(a_i|c)$ where d is the number of attributes in the set a.

Random Forest (RF). Ensemble methods are popular classification tools. They are based on the idea of generating multiple predictors used in combination to classify new unseen samples. We use a random forest which combines bagging for each tree with random feature selection at each node to split the data, thus generating multiple decision tree classifiers. Each decision tree gives its own opinion on test sample classification. The prediction is made by taking a majority vote among the decision tree classifiers.

Support Vector Machine (SVM). SVMs work by finding a separating margin that maximizes the geometric distance between classes [29]. The separating margin is termed the hyperplane.

Logistic Regression (LOG-REG). Logistic regression classifies samples by computing the odds ratio. The odds ratio gives the strength of association between the attributes and the class.

4.3.2 Semisupervised Approaches

Labeling data is expensive and often requires expert domain knowledge. Semi-supervised approaches work with limited labeled data by leveraging information from the unlabeled data during the training period. That is, instead of building a model with only labeled data like in supervised learning, semi-supervised learning leverages both labeled and unlabeled data during the training phase. So, for our case, not only do we use the data with ground-truth labels from the security analyst, but we also use the unlabeled data we have to build semi-supervised models, just as in the supervised learning case, the classification challenge is to predict whether a given product or thread is hacking related. We discuss popular semi-supervised approaches used in this work.

Label propagation (LP). Label propagation [119] has been widely used for semi-supervised classification task [11, 62, 114, 22]. It estimates the label values based on graph Laplacian [8] where the model is represented by a weighted graph $G = (V, E)$, with V (the vertices) representing the samples and E (the weighted edges) indicating the similarity between samples. A subset of these vertices are labeled and these vertices are then used to estimate the labels of the remaining, unlabeled vertices under the assumption that the edges are able to capture the similarity between samples. Hence the performance of these methods depends on the similarity measure used. The most commonly used similarity measures include k-NN and Gaussian kernel.

Co-training (CT). Co-training was proposed by Blum and Mitchell [13] and works by dividing the feature set into two distinct sets of features, which are assumed to be independent. Two classifiers are trained with the labeled set of samples, denoted by L. These trained classifiers are then used to estimate the labels for the unlabeled points. High-confidence predicted labels estimated from classifier-1 are added to the labeled set L of classifier-2 and vice versa. Every time the labeled set L is updated, the classifiers are retrained. This procedure is repeated until all of the unlabeled points have received labels or no new samples exceed the confidence threshold. Informally, this method can be viewed as two classifiers "teaching" each other. For this approach to work, it is necessary that the two classifiers have distinct views of the samples, meaning that the two features sets are uncorrelated and that each classifier is able to make an independent decision on a sample. In our cotraining experiments, we used a confidence threshold of 70% and implemented the algorithm using various classifiers in order to compare performance. The results for these experiments can be seen in Section 4.3.3.2.

Latent Dirichlet Allocation (LDA). Latent Dirichlet Allocation is an unsupervised modeling technique, with a goal of inferring a fixed number of topics present in a corpus of documents. Additionally, LDA will provide a distribution over the learned topics that are present in a given document. Each topic can be represented by its representative words (see Table 4.5) and each document will receive a different unique distribution over the learned topics. For example, a document might receive a topic distribution consisting of 25% topic 1, 75% topic 2, and 0% topic 3 (assuming LDA was configured to learn 3 topics). We can use the distribution over topics as features for a classifier, and thus LDA can be used as a dimensionality reduction technique [12].

4.3.3 Experiments: Marketplaces

The recent growth in popularity of darknet marketplaces provides a new avenue to gather information about the cyber threat landscape. As stated earlier, these marketplaces often sell goods and services that do not relate to malicious hacking, including drugs, pornography, weapons, and nonhacking-related software services. Only a small fraction of products (13% in this chapter's dataset) are related to malicious hacking. We thus require a model that can reliably filter out the irrelevant (i.e., not hacking-related) products. The data collected from exploit marketplaces is noisy and hence not suitable to use directly as input to a learning model, meaning several steps of preprocessing and data cleaning are required. We now discuss the challenges associated with the marketplace product dataset and the data-processing steps taken to address them. Note that similar challenges had to be addressed for hacker forum and subreddit data.

4.3.3.1 Classification Challenges

Text Cleaning. Product titles and descriptions on marketplaces often have a significant amount of text that serves as noise to the classifier (e.g., **SALE**). To deal with these instances, we first removed all nonalphanumeric characters from a product's title and description. This, in tandem with standard stop-word removal, greatly improved classification performance.

Misspellings and Word Variations. Misspellings, which is an obstacle for the standard bag-of-words feature representation, frequently occur on forums and marketplaces. Additionally, with the standard bag-of-words approach, variations of words are considered separately (e.g. hacker, hack, hackers, etc.). Word stemming and lemmatization mitigates the issue of word variations, but fails to fix the issue of misspellings in most cases. To address this, we turn to character n-gram features. As an example of character n-gram features, consider the word "hacker." If we were using tri-gram character features, the word "hacker" would yield the features "hac," "ack," "cke," "ker." The benefit of this is that the variations or misspellings of the word in the forms "hack," "hackz," "hackker," will all yield some common features. We found that using character n-grams in the range (3, 7) outperformed word stemming in our experiments.

Large Feature Space. In the standard bag-of-words feature-extraction approach, the feature matrix gets very large as the number of words increase. Consider the case where the training corpus contains 100,000 unique words and 10,000 documents. The feature matrix then has 100,000 entries for each document, meaning that there are 1 billion entries in the feature matrix. As the number of unique words and documents grow, this bloated feature matrix begins to greatly increase training time, as the feature matrix can quickly become too large to fit in memory. Using n-gram features further increases the already oversized feature matrix. To address this issue, we leveraged the sparse matrix data structure in the scipy[1] library, which takes advantage of the fact that most of these over 1 billion entries in the feature matrix will be zero. That is, if a word or n-gram feature is not present in a given document, there is simply no entry for that feature in the sparse matrix, so no additional memory will be used. Switching from a dense matrix representation to a sparse matrix representation greatly reduced runtime; using the dense matrix representation was hardly tractable for even a few hundred documents.

Preserving Title Feature Context. As the title and description of a product are disjoint, we found that simply concatenating the description to the title before extracting features led to suboptimal classification performance. We believe that by doing a simple concatenation, we were losing important contextual information, as there may be features that should be interpreted differently should they appear in the title versus in the description. Initially, to rectify this issue, we used two separate classifiers: one for the title and one for the description. With this construction, when an unknown product was being classified, we would pass the title features to the title classifier and the description features to the description classifier. If either classifier returned a positive classification, we would assign the product a positive classification. However, we believe

---

[1] http://www.scipy.org/

Table 4.2. *Markets and number of products collected*

Markets	Products	Markets	Products
Market-1	439	Market-6	497
Market-2	1329	Market-7	491
Market-3	455	Market-8	764
Market-4	4018	Market-9	2014
Market-5	876	Market-10	600

that this again led to the loss of important contextual information. To fix this, we independently extracted character n-gram features from the title string and description string, which yields a title feature vector and a description feature vector. We then horizontally concatenated these vectors, forming a single-feature vector which includes separate features for the title and description.

4.3.3.2 Results
We considered 10 marketplaces to train and test our learning model. A summary of the data from these marketplaces is shown in Table 4.2. With the help of security analysts, we labeled 25% of the products from each marketplace. Table 4.3 gives an example of products along with their ground truth labels assigned by security analysts.

The experimental setup is as follows. We perform a leave-one-marketplace-out cross-validation. In other words, given n marketplaces we train on $n - 1$ and test on the remaining one. We repeat this experiment for each of the marketplaces. For the supervised experiments, we only use the labeled data (25% of its products) from each marketplace. We evaluate the performance based primarily on three metrics: precision, recall, and unbiased F1. Precision, in this case, is the fraction of the products that were classified as relevant that were actually relevant. Recall is the fraction of relevant products that were classified

Table 4.3. *Example of products*

Product title	Relevant
20+ Hacking Tools (Botnets Keyloggers Worms and More!)	YES
SQLI DUMPER V 7.0 SQL INJECTION SCANNER	YES
Amazon Receipt Generator	NO
5 gm Colombian Cocaine	NO

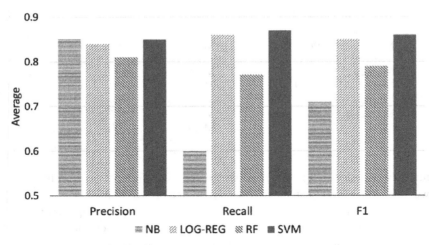

Figure 4.3.   Average precision, recall and F1 comparisons for NB, LOG-REG, RF and SVM for supervised product classification.

as relevant by the model. The results are averaged and weighted by the number of samples in each market. F1 is the harmonic mean of precision and recall. For this application, high recall is desirable as we do not want to unintentionally filter-out relevant products. In the supervised approach, SVM with linear kernel performed the best, recalling 87% of the relevant products while maintaining a precision of 85% (Figure 4.3). SVM's performance was likely due to the fact that it maximizes generality as opposed to minimizing error.

As stated, only 25% of the data is labeled, as labeling often requires expert domain knowledge and can be time consuming. However, this significant cost and time investment can be reduced by applying a semisupervised approach, which leverages the large amount of unlabeled data to aid in classification. The semisupervised experimental setup is similar to the supervised setup, but this time we also utilize the unlabeled data from each marketplace (75%) for training.

Figure 4.4 shows the performance comparison for various semi-supervised approaches. For the cotraining approach, we divided the feature space into two sets, both based on character n-grams. For these experiments, we split the feature space directly in half, though another logical split of the feature space would have been between the title features and the description features, giving us two views of the same sample. Cotraining with Linear SVM was able to recall 92% of the relevant products while maintaining a precision of 82%. In

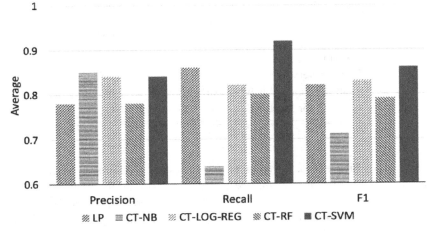

Figure 4.4.   Average precision, recall and F1 comparisons for LP, CT-NB, CT-LOG-REG, CT-RF and CT-SVM for semi-supervised product classification.

this case, the unlabeled data aided the classification in improving the recall to 92% without significantly reducing the precision, as compared to the supervised approach.

4.3.4 Experiment: Forums

In addition to the darknet/deepnet marketplaces that we have already discussed, there are also numerous darknet forums on which users discuss a variety of topics, including malicious hacking. Again, there is the issue that only a fraction of these forum threads contain information that is relevant to malicious hacking or the trading of exploits. Hence, we need a classifier to identify relevant (i.e., hacking-related) threads. This classification problem is very similar to the product classification problem previously discussed, with a similar set of challenges.

We performed evaluation on an English forum and a Russian forum. For the English forum we considered a dataset of 781 topics with 5373 posts. Table 4.4 gives examples of forum thread topics that received analyst labels as being relevant or not. We labeled 25% of the thread topics and performed a 10-fold cross validation with various supervised and semisupervised techniques. In the supervised setting, LOG-REG performed the best with 80% precision and

Table 4.4. *Example of topics*

Topic	Relevant
Bitcoin Mixing services	YES
Hacking service	YES
I can vend cannabis where should I go?	NO
Looking for MDE/MDEA shipped to Aus	NO

68% recall (Figure 4.5). Leveraging unlabeled data in semi-supervised techniques was able to improve the recall while maintaining the precision, with LOG-REG co-training improving the recall to 80% and precision to 78%.

We also tried our classification approach on forums in languages other than English. Many of the non-English forums like Russian use English words to describe hacking techniques and exploits (e.g., "RAT" and "botnet"). Hence, we use the same character n-gram features for the Russian forum too. For evaluation we considered a Russian forum with 1609 forum thread topics, containing a total of 8961 posts. We had 25% of the topics labeled by a Russian speaking security analyst. The comparison of performance amongst the various classification techniques is shown in Figure 4.6. Note that, in this case, the supervised approaches outperformed the semi-supervised approaches.

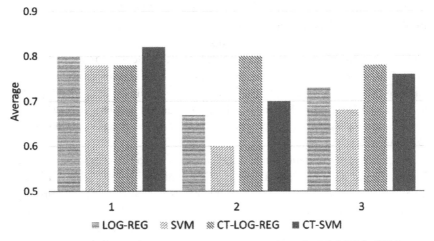

Figure 4.5.   Average precision, recall and F1 comparisons for LOG-REG, SVM, CT-LOG-REG, and CT-SVM for English forum topic classification.

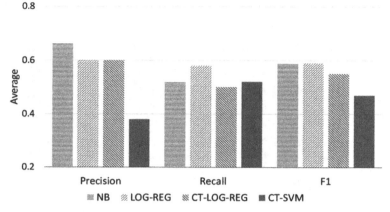

Figure 4.6.   Average precision, recall and F1 comparisons for NB, LOG-REG, CT-LOG-REG and CT-SVM for Russian forum topic classification.

LOG-REG had the best recall, at 58%, with a precision of 60%. We are exploring a combination of machine learning and keyword filtering to improve the performance on foreign language forums.

4.3.5 Experiment: Subreddits

We also crawled data from subreddits, where there have been instances of users discussing darknet and deepnet websites. This can be viewed as meta-discussion about the darknet marketplaces and forums. But, just as in the case of marketplaces/forum, not all subreddit threads are relevant to malicious hacking, exploit markets, or hacker forums. Thus, we again need a classifier to identify the threads of interest. For evaluating our models, we utilized 1550 topics (threads) containing a total of 8000 posts from 33 different subreddits. We, again, label 25% of the topics and used these labeled samples to perform a 10-fold cross validation. Figure 4.7 shows the two best performing supervised methods (NB and LOG-REG). Naive Bayes is able to recall 68% of the relevant subreddits with a precision of 53%.

We again saw an improvement from the semisupervised approaches. Figure 4.7 shows the two best performing semisupervised methods (CT-LOG-REG and CT-SVM) and two best supervised methods. Here, the 10-fold cross validation is performed only on the labeled points. Cotraining with linear SVM performs the best with an average precision of 74%, recalling 68% of the subreddits.

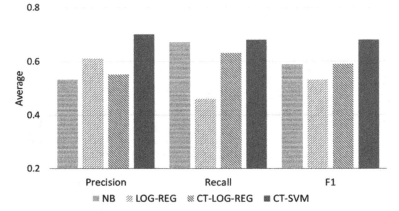

Figure 4.7.   Average precision, recall and F1 comparisons for LP, CT-LOG-REG, CT-RF and CT-SVM for subreddits.

4.3.6 Darknet New Page Discovery

The crawler often encounters new web links while crawling data from forums and subreddits. These new links might point to new marketplaces or forums relating to malicious hacking, and we want to automate the process of determining whether or not a given new webpage is relevant to our data collection efforts. For the previous classification problems we were able to rely on the structure of the input. That is, in the case of the product and forum classifiers we knew that we were receiving only a product/forum thread title and description/post information. This classification problem is different. The input is a single HTML page, the structure of which is completely unknown. With only this information, the classifier then has to determine if the page is relevant or not. Without any assumption on structure, it is very difficult to extract only the parts of the page that are relevant. In the preprocessing step, we extract all visible text on the page (including header, footer, sidebar, menu etc.).

In our first approach, we used a bag-of-words approach with TF-IDF (term frequency—inverse document frequency) on the extracted text (i.e., all visible text on the webpage). Using this approach, when given two pages from the same website, both pages will have an identical header, footer, sidebar, menu, etc. One difficulty here was that the term frequencies of the words in the header, footer, etc. are not necessarily that important for classification, which generates a lot of noise in the feature space. With TF-IDF-based features, we found that the classifiers greatly overfit to the pages that were in the positive training set and, as a result, pages from new sites were nearly always classified as negative—regardless of content. To help mitigate the problem of overfitting the model to pages in the training set, we used the topic-distribution generated by Latent Dirichlet Allocation (LDA) [12] as features, rather than TF-IDF or bag-of-words, which greatly improved performance on an independent evaluation set. In our ongoing work, we are examining additional features beyond those based on text.

4.3.6.1 Results

For training our model, we use all the positive webpages from marketplaces and forums already identified as relevant by an analyst. The negative pages were gathered by an analyst during their search for relevant darknet and deepnet websites. Using all of the labeled pages as a training set we trained two Linear SVM models, one with TF-IDF features and one with LDA topic distribution features, with word stemming done in both cases. To evaluate the models, a security analyst provided us with a list of links. The links were crawled, yielding 2855 HTML pages with unknown content. Hence, the evaluation described in this section was a true validation set. Our focus is on precision with the intuition that the classifier can point out a relatively small number of pages that are likely to be relevant to the analyst.

TF-IDF-Based Results. When using standard TF-IDF as features, only 35 pages were classified as relevant, with only three unique sites represented, two of which were deemed irrelevant by an analyst and the third site having pages that appeared in the training set. In other words, using TF-IDF features yielded no pages from new markets.

LDA-Based Results. LDA greatly improved performance on the evaluation set. When evaluating a Linear SVM model with LDA topic distribution features, trained on the labeled data, 58 of the 2855 unlabeled pages were given a positive classification. Of the 58 pages, the analyst deemed 50 of them as relevant to what they typically look for, with seven new markets represented in the set of 58 pages. This classifier performed far better at extracting the "market structure," as nearly all positively classified pages were from darknet markets. Once markets have been identified, we can leverage the market product classifier discussed previously to only extract products relating to malicious hacking. We also note that the LDA topics themselves are useful to the analyst—especially as topics evolve over time. Table 4.5 shows a sample of the 25 LDA topics that were used in this experiment.

Table 4.5. *A sample of positive topics*

1. bitcoin, use, address, account, order, contact, email, service, product, please, day, send, market, new, make, share, time, free, month
2. price, day, ago, item, usd, btc, fix, quantity, buy, view, left, bid, unlimited, software, book, ms, fraud, secure, exploit
3. service, onion, hidden, tor, bitcoin, forum, wiki, host, link, card, market, directory, clearnet, site, drug, web, marketplace

4.4 Related Work

Web crawling is a popular way of collecting large amounts of data from the Internet. In many applications, researchers are interested in specific topics for their application, and hence there is a need for a topic-based (or focused) crawler [19, 18]. Most previously designed focused crawlers were designed to collect information from the *surface web*, with little concentration on darknet websites. More recently, a focused crawler designed to crawl the darknet [37] was built and used to research darknet forums, collecting data over a period of time and then performing static analysis to study the online communities. The authors also used different data-mining techniques for these forums in [20]. We, on the other hand, not only look at darknet forums but also collect information from exploit marketplaces hosting a range of products relating to malicious hacking.

Additionally, web-crawlers have been developed to aid law enforcement to track online extremist activities [74]. This work has included the use of a self-guided web-crawler using sentiment analysis to identify extremist content, threats to critical infrastructure [68] and online sexual child exploitation [116]. Another application of leveraging darknet information to counter human trafficking was developed by DARPA through the Memex program[2]—a program with different goals than the work described in this chapter. Our previous work leverages the exploit information from marketplaces in a game theoretic framework to formulate system configurations that minimize the potential damage of a malicious cyber-attack [90], which will be discussed in detail in Chapter 6.

4.5 Conclusion

In this chapter, we discussed the implementation of a system for cyber threat intelligence gathering, which relies on mined data from the darknet. At the time

---

[2] http://opencatalog.darpa.mil/MEMEX.html

of writing, we are transitioning this system to commercial partners. For our data collection, we considered social platforms on the darknet and the deepnet and addressed various design challenges to develop a focused crawler using data-mining and machine-learning techniques.

In the next chapter, we will discuss how we can apply unsupervised learning techniques to this data to further analyze hacker marketplaces, providing more useful threat intelligence and shedding some light on the threat landscape. The data-collection pipeline presented here allows us to build sophisticated threat intelligence analysis models on top of the darknet data. Chapters 6 and 7 discuss such analysis models.

5

Analyzing Products and Vendors in Malicious Hacking Markets

5.1 Introduction

Chapter 3 introduced darknet hacker communities and marketplaces, with Chapter 4 presenting a system for gathering data from these sites. In this chapter, we extend the work from [70], presenting techniques to analyze the aggregated dataset, with a goal of providing rich cyber threat intelligence. We identify and analyze users that participate in multiple online communities, look at some of the high-priced zero-day exploits for sale, discuss how government-assigned vulnerability identifiers are used to indicate a product's target, and use unsupervised learning to categorize and study the product offerings of 17 darknet marketplaces. For product categorization, we use a combination of manual labeling with clustering techniques to identify specific categories. Through a series of case studies showcasing various findings relating to malicious hacker behavior, we hope to illustrate the utility of these cyber threat intelligence tools.

The price of a given product on a darknet marketplace is typically indicated in Bitcoin. The BTC to USD conversion rate is highly volatile. At the time of writing, the Bitcoin to USD conversion rate was $649.70 to 1 BTC, whereas during the experiments discussed during this chapter, which occurred only a few months prior to the writing of this book, the conversion rate was $380.03 to 1 BTC.

The goal of a cyber threat intelligence system is to aid cybersecurity professionals with their strategic cyber-defense planning and to address questions such as:

1 *What vendors and users have a presence in multiple darknet/deepnet markets/forums?*
2 *What zero-day exploits are being developed by malicious hackers?*

Table 5.1. *Scraped data from marketplaces in the Darkweb*

Marketplaces	17
Products (total)	16122
Products (distinct)	9093
Vendors	1332

3 *What vulnerabilities do the latest exploits target?*
4 *What types of products are exclusive to certain vendors and markets?*

After aggregating the hacking-related products and hacking-related discussions from a number of darknet marketplaces and forums, respectively, we can begin answering these questions via an in-depth analysis of the data in order to provide a better understanding of the interactions within and between these communities.

5.2 Marketplace Data Characteristics

In this section, we describe the dataset used in this chapter. We examined the hacking-related products from 17 darknet marketplaces, finding many products that were cross-posted between markets, often by vendors of the same username. Figure 5.1 shows the count of vendors using the same screen-name across multiple marketplaces and Table 5.1 displays the dataset statistics, after removing duplicates (cross-posts). Note that about 57% of products are unique by simple (string ordinal) comparison methods. We see a power-law trend in the number of vendors that sell identical products, with 77% of the 9,093 distinct products being sold exclusively by one vendor, as seen in Figure 5.3.

5.3 Users Having Presence in Markets/Forums

Previous studies on darkweb crawling [37, 9] explore a single darknet domain, namely hacker forums. In this section, we create a social network that includes data from both marketplaces and forums, which allows us to study cross-site connections. With member usernames, which we found in Chapter 3 to be consistent across platforms for purposes of building reputation and product advertising, we are able to produce a connected graph of users in each community. A subgraph of this network is shown in Figure 5.2. Using these integrated graphic representations, one can visualize an individual's participation in both domains,

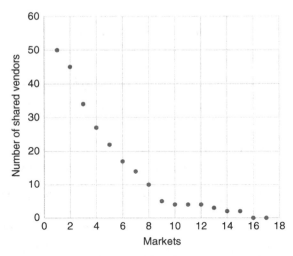

Figure 5.1.   Distribution of shared vendors over markets.

leading to a better comprehension of the malicious hacker networks and helping in determining social groups within these communities. The presence of users on multiple markets and forums follows a power law, as seen in Figure 5.4. There are 1521 users who are present on two or more platforms; Figure 5.5 considers one such user/vendor who is active in 7 marketplaces and 1 forum, offering 361 malicious hacking related products, and discussing these products on a hacker forum. With an average rating of 4.7/5.0, as rated by customers on the marketplaces, and with more than 8500 successful transactions, this vendor is quite active.

5.4 Discovery of Zero-Day Exploits

Over a 4-week period, we detected 16 claimed zero-day exploits from the marketplace data. Zero-day exploits are exploits that leverage vulnerabilities not publicly released by the product manufacturer. For this reason, they go for a premium in the markets. Table 5.2 shows a sample of zero-day exploits with their selling price in Bitcoin. The Android WebView zero-day utilizes a vulnerability in the rendering of webpages in Android devices, affecting devices running on Android 4.3 Jelly Bean or earlier versions of the operating system, which comprised more than 60% of the Android devices in 2015. After the original posting of this zero-day, a patch was released in Android KitKat 4.4 and Lollipop 5.0. As not all users will update to the new operating system, the exploit

Table 5.2. *Example of zero-day exploits*

Zero-day exploit	Price (BTC)
Internet Explorer 11 Remote Code Execution 0day	20.4676
Android WebView 0day RCE	40.8956
Fresh 0day MS Office	38.3436

continues to be sold for a high price. Detection of these zero-day exploits at an early stage can help organizations minimize the damage of a potential attack on their system, by informing them of potentially vulnerable software in their organization.

Figure 5.2. Vendor-market-forum social network.

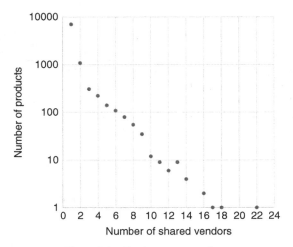

Figure 5.3.   Products over vendors.

5.5 Exploits Targeting Known Vulnerabilities

Zero-day vulnerabilities are difficult to discover, and hence zero-day exploits are rare. Exploits targeting known vulnerabilities are often for sale on these darknet markets. These exploits are advertised as targeting specific vulnerabilities in a piece of software, and sometimes vendors mention Common Vulnerability and Exposure (CVE) numbers assigned by the National Institute of

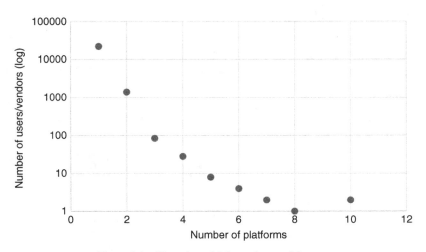

Figure 5.4.   Users in multiple markets and forums.

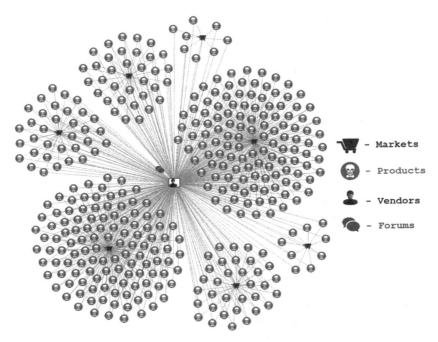

Figure 5.5.   A centric network of a vendor.

Standards and Technology (NIST). Using NIST's National Vulnerability Database (NVD),[1] we can uniquely identify the specific versions of software that an exploit targets via an assigned CVE number. For instance, the Silent Doc exploit allows remote attackers to execute arbitrary code or cause a denial of service (memory corruption), affecting specific versions of Microsoft Word. Additionally, for products that list CVE numbers, we can identify the severity level associated with a given exploit/vulnerability. NVD assigns a severity level of HIGH to the vulnerability associated with the Silent Doc exploit.

Exploit kits often cite many CVE numbers and hence target multiple vulnerabilities. The Xer Exploit Kit (Table 5.3), for example, cites 7 unique CVE numbers.

5.6 Identifying Specific Product Categories

The ability to identify product-types that are exclusive to specific vendors and markets would be particularly valuable in analysis of these online communities.

---

[1] https://nvd.nist.gov/home.cfm

Table 5.3. *Exploit-vulnerability*

Exploit	Vulnerability	
SILENT DOC EXPLOIT	CVE-2014-1761	
Sqlninja	CVE-2010-0232	
Xer Exploit Kit / traffic /	CVE-2015-2426	CVE-2015-0313
LOADS	CVE-2015-0311	CVE-2014-0556
	CVE-2015-0317	CVE-2014-0515
	CVE-2015-2444	

We use a combination of manual labeling and clustering techniques to cluster the products into distinct categories.

5.6.1 Clustering Approach

In order to maximize cluster purity, we experimented with a variety of feature extraction techniques. To determine the best technique, we manually categorized 500 products into 34 distinct product categories (listed in Table 5.5). Using 400 of the categorized products, we generated 34 centroids via K-Means, evaluating the resulting clusters on the remaining 100 samples using the Rand-index metric [87]. Rand-index is defined as the number of pairs correctly considered in the same class or correctly considered in different classes divided by $\binom{n}{2}$, where n is the number of samples. Additionally, we use standard entropy, which measures the amount of disorder in a cluster, to examine the purity of the clusters. Formally, entropy is defined as:

$$entropy(D_i) = -\sum_{j=1}^{k} Pr_i(c_j) \log_2 Pr_i(c_j), \tag{5.1}$$

where $Pr_i(c_j)$ is the proportion of class c_j data points in cluster D_i, and k is the number of clusters. The total entropy (considering all clusters) is:

$$entropy_{total}(D) = \sum_{i=1}^{k} \frac{|D_i|}{|D|} entropy(D_i) \tag{5.2}$$

Table 5.4 shows the performance of each vectorization technique, with respect to Rand-index and entropy. Cosine similarity with character n-grams in the range 3 to 4, 3 to 5, and 3 to 6, yielded the best results for Rand-index (0.986) and entropy (0.067). As the machine-learning techniques from Chapter 4 do not perfectly recall all hacking-related products, we examined products that were initially classified as nonhacking related, but had a cosine similarity of less than 0.1 from the K-Means centroids, in hopes of identifying additional nonhacking-related products that may have slipped past our classifier. There were 410 such products, which were manually examined and were found to be irrelevant to our target domain. Finding that character n-gram features were more discriminative than bag-of-words or bi-grams validated the choice of feature extraction technique for our classification pipeline in Chapter 4.

5.6.2 Analyst Interpretation of Product Clusters

In this section, we examine the product category clusters that were found. In order to analyze these clusters, we compute entropy with respect to two different criteria: marketplaces and vendors. By doing this, we were able to identify which product categories are exclusive to which vendors and marketplaces. A low marketplace entropy for a given cluster indicates that the products within this category are more exclusive to a few marketplaces. Similarly, a low vendor entropy indicates the cluster's products are sold primarily by a few vendors (perhaps even one). Table 5.5 lists the aforementioned entropy results.

As seen in Table 5.5, the *Links* cluster, which corresponds to products concerning links and referrals to other darknet hacking sites, has the lowest entropy with respect to marketplaces. This suggests that the majority of link-related products come from the same market. After further investigation, we found that 80% of link-related products came from two markets. However, vendor entropy for this same cluster is much higher, indicating that though link-related products reside within only a few marketplaces, within these marketplaces there are a number of vendors selling these products.

Similarly, the *Hacking Tools* cluster has the lowest vendor entropy, indicating that only a few vendors sell these types of hacking tools. Indeed, we find that two vendors sell 416 (50%) of the products in this cluster. At first glance, it might be surprising to find that these two vendors sell the majority of this type of hacking tool, however, we find that these two vendors are actually organizations and use similar language in all of their product description in an effort to brand their wares.

The *Facebook* and *Keylogger* clusters are examples of product clusters with high entropy, as products related to these categories are sold by many vendors on many marketplaces. For example, in cluster *Facebook*, there were 119 products from 67 vendors, and the most prolific vendor with respect to this cluster authored only 8 products regarding Facebook-related hacking and spamming. In this cluster, products were distributed across 15 markets, and the most well-represented market was associated with 30 products. With a large

Table 5.4. *K-means evaluation (fixed centroids)*

	Word(1,1)	Word(1,2)	Char(3,4)	Char(3,5)	Char(3,6)	Char(3,7)	Char(4,4)	Char(4,5)	Char(4,6)	Char(4,7)
Rand-index										
Cosine	0.986	0.985	0.986	0.986	0.986	0.985	0.985	0.985	0.984	0.982
Euclidean	0.986	0.977	0.976	0.973	0.973	0.974	0.975	0.975	0.977	0.971
Entropy										
Cosine	0.075	0.079	0.067	0.067	0.067	0.075	0.072	0.079	0.088	0.088
Euclidean	0.224	0.110	0.153	0.156	0.156	0.141	0.134	0.134	0.137	0.175

Table 5.5. *Clusters entropy*

Rank	Cluster name	Nº products	Nº markets	Market entropy	Nº vendors	Vendor entropy
1	Carding	1263	16	0.320	315	0.720
2	PayPal-related	1103	16	0.340	335	0.754
3	Cashing credit cards	867	16	0.351	256	0.738
4	PGP	865	15	0.347	203	0.696
5	Netflix-related	846	14	0.270	351	0.805
6	Hacking tools—general	825	15	0.331	132	0.516
7	Dumps—general	749	12	0.289	280	0.777
8	Linux-related	561	16	0.372	117	0.758
9	Email hacking tools	547	13	0.335	196	0.738
10	Network security tools	539	15	0.366	117	0.621
11	Ebay-related	472	15	0.385	163	0.772
12	Amazon-related	456	16	0.391	197	0.825
13	Bitcoin	443	15	0.360	201	0.823
14	Links (lists)	422	12	0.211	221	0.838
15	Banking	384	13	0.349	186	0.840
16	Point of Sale	375	15	0.384	181	0.841
17	VPN	272	12	0.413	130	0.827
18	Botnet	257	12	0.291	110	0.796
19	Hacking groups invitation	251	14	0.387	143	0.865
20	RATs	249	15	0.453	99	0.797
21	Browser-related	249	12	0.380	134	0.857
22	Physical layer hacking	237	13	0.408	122	0.856
23	Password cracking	230	13	0.434	100	0.781
24	Smartphone—general	223	14	0.408	110	0.816
25	Wireless hacking	222	13	0.389	56	0.601
26	Phishing	218	13	0.403	111	0.849
27	Exploit kits	218	14	0.413	91	0.795
28	Viruses/counter antivirus	210	14	0.413	60	0.684
29	Network layer hacking	205	14	0.459	60	0.716
30	RDP servers	191	12	0.405	124	0.895
31	Android-related	156	11	0.429	60	0.770
32	Keyloggers	143	13	0.496	77	0.862
33	Windows-related	119	12	0.464	50	0.717
34	Facebook-related	119	15	0.501	67	0.876

supply of Facebook-related products spread across many markets and vendors, we conclude that there must be significant demand for social media related hacking and phishing tools. We see similar statistics for keylogging products, which is consistent with the known widespread prevalence of keyloggers.

5.7 Conclusion

In this chapter we conducted an initial examination of malware products from 17 malicious hacker markets. We saw a number of case studies that illustrate how the darknet data can be used to provide useful cyber threat intelligence. Through unsupervised clustering techniques, we were able to identify specific product categories, which yielded several interesting characteristics of certain product-types, including exclusivity to specific markets and vendors. At the time of writing, we are examining other methods for grouping products, which include using matrix factorization and supervised techniques. Additionally, we are studying the underlying social network of vendors through relationships based on similar product offerings.

In the next chapter we will present another technique to provide actionable intelligence, introducing a game theoretic model that pits a system administrator against an attacker that is armed with exploits from these darknet markets. Both Chapters 6 and 7 introduce more sophisticated models that use the aggregated data from the darknet in interesting ways to provide rich threat intelligence.

6

Using Game Theory for Threat Intelligence

6.1 Introduction

Penetration testing is regarded as the gold-standard for understanding how well an organization can withstand sophisticated cyber-attacks. In a penetration test, a "red team" is hired to expose major flaws in the firm's security infrastructure. Recently, however, the market for exploit kits has continued to evolve and what was once a rather hard-to-penetrate and exclusive market—whose buyers were primarily western governments [95], has now become more accessible to a much wider population. In particular, 2015 saw the introduction of darknet markets specializing in zero-day exploit kits—exploits designed to leverage previously undiscovered vulnerabilities. These markets, which were discussed in Chapters 3–5, make exploits widely available to potential attackers. These exploit kits are difficult and time consuming to develop—and are often sold at premium prices. The cost associated with these sophisticated kits generally precludes penetration testers from simply obtaining such exploits, meaning an alternative approach is needed to understand what exploits an attacker will most likely purchase and how to defend against them. In this chapter, we introduce a data-driven security game framework to model an attacker and a defender of a specific system, providing system-specific policy recommendations to the defender. In addition to providing a formal framework and algorithms to develop strategies, we present experimental results from applying our framework, for various system configurations, on a subset of the real-world exploit data gathered from the system presented in Chapter 4. This game theoretic framework provides another example of rich cyber threat intelligence that can be derived from the darknet exploit data.

For this chapter, we surveyed 8 unique marketplaces and show some example exploit kits from the data set in Table 6.1. The widespread availability of

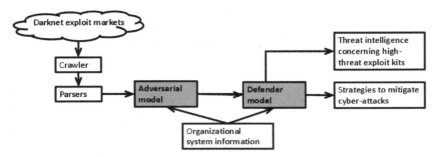

Figure 6.1.   Schematic of real-time exploit analysis system.

zero-day exploits represents a potential game changer for penetration testers—
specifically posing the following questions:

- *What exploits will an attacker likely purchase if he targets my organization?*
- *What software used in the organization pose the biggest risk to new threats?*

To address these challenging questions, we extend a data-driven security
game framework, initially introduced in [90]. Given a system configuration (or
a distribution of system configurations within an organization) we model an
attacker who, given a budget, will purchase exploits to maximize his level of
access to the target system. Likewise, a defender will look to adjust system
configurations in an effort to minimize the effectiveness of an attacker while
ensuring that necessary software dependencies are satisfied. Not only have we
introduced a rigorous and thoroughly analyzed framework for these problems,
but we have also implemented and evaluated a system that is fed with real-
world exploit data. At the time of writing, we are pushing to more closely
integrate this framework with the crawling and scraping system presented in
Chapter 4, with a goal of providing real-time game-theoretic assessment of the
exploit market—while considering specific system information. We provide a
schematic diagram of our system in Figure 6.1. This chapter includes a security
game framework designed to model an attacker with access to exploit markets
and a defender of information technology infrastructure (Section 6.2), theoretical analysis of the framework (Section 6.3) leading to the development of
algorithms to find near-optimal strategies for both players (Section 6.4), and
an implementation of the system and the results of a thorough suite of experiments on real-world data (Section 6.5). Before discussing these contributions,
we review some domain-specific background and related literature on security
games.

Table 6.1. *Example of products in dataset*

Product	Price in BTC	Price in $*
GovRAT (Source Code + 1 Code Signing Certificate Included)	2.000	$456.92
0day Wordpress MU Remote Shell	1.500	$342.69
A5/1 Encryption Rainbow Tables	1.500	$342.69
Unlimited Code Signing Certificate	1.200	$274.16
Ready-made Linux botnet 600 SERVERS	1.200	$274.16
FUD version of Adobe Flash <=16.0.0.287 (CVE 2015-0311)	2.626	$600.00

* Price in US dollars at time of data collection [1 BTC = $228.46].

Exploit markets on the darknet. While criminal activity on the darknet has been extensively studied over the past decade for issues such as drug trade [102] and terrorism [20] the markets of exploits existing on the darknet are much less well understood. There has been related work on malicious hacker forums [118, 64], which did not focus on the purchase and sale of specific items. Markets of malicious products relevant to cybersecurity have been previously studied [2, 94], but none of these works gathered data on specific exploits (or other products) from either the darkweb or open Internet; nor did they examine the markets through the lens of security games. To our knowledge [90], the work that this chapter extend is the first work that describes the collection of price data on specific exploits for sale on the darkweb and then analyzes them in a security game framework that yields policy recommendations for cyber defenders that are tailored to specific system configurations.

Related work in security games. In recent years, "security games" where attacker-defender models are used to inform the actions of defenders in military, law-enforcement, and homeland security applications have gained much traction (see [107] for an overview). With regard to cybersecurity, there have been many contributions including intrusion detection [79], attack graph based games [66], and honeypot placement [56]. However, to the best of our knowledge, [90] and [89] represent the first game theoretic approaches to *host-based* defense where the activities of the attacker are informed from an "unconventional" source (information not directly related to the defender's system)— specifically information from darknet markets in this case. Further, the very recent emergence of darknet markets specializing in zero-day exploits allow for the integration of information that was unavailable in previous work.

6.2 Security Game Framework

Here we formalize our concept of our security game where the attacker is a malicious hacker with access to darknet exploit markets and the defender is tasked with host-based defense of either a single or group of systems. We use the notation V to represent the entire set of vulnerabilities within a given computer system. Though there may be vulnerabilities not yet detected by the system administrator, we can mine for information on new vulnerabilities through an examination of darknet hacking markets. In a real-world organization, system administrators are not able to patch all vulnerabilities for a variety of reasons. Software dependencies, use of legacy systems, and non-availability of patches are some examples. To model this, we define a "constraint set" (denoted C) as a subset of V. The vulnerabilities in a constraint set represent the vulnerabilities required for some system functionality. When each vulnerability in a constraint set C is in the presented attack surface (i.e., externally accessible), C is then said to be satisfied and the system supports the functionality modeled by C. Let $\mathbf{C}$ represent the set of all possible constraint sets. We extend this idea with an "application constraint set," which, for an arbitrary application, i, denoted C_i, is a set of constraint sets (i.e., $C_i \subseteq \mathbf{C}$). Each constraint set in C_i represents a set of vulnerabilities that together will provide complete functionality of application i. C_i is said to be satisfied if any single constraint set in C_i is satisfied. If C_i is satisfied by a system configuration, and hence at least one constraint set in C_i is satisfied, application i will properly operate on the system. $\mathcal{C}$ is the set of all application constraint sets for a given system configuration and represents all of the applications to be run on the system. So, in this framework, for a given system, a system administrator must select which vulnerabilities must be present in order to allow each application i to function. This begs the question as to how to make this selection—so we now start to define some concepts relevant to the adversary.

We will use ex to denote a particular exploit—a technique used to take advantage of a given vulnerability. Let Ex denote the set of all possible exploits and $\mathbf{Ex}$ denote the set of all possible exploit sets (i.e., $\mathbf{Ex} = 2^{Ex}$). For each $ex \in Ex$, c_{ex} is the associated cost of exploit ex—and this is specified directly on a darknet market (normally in Bitcoin). Associated with the set of exploits is the Exploit Function, ExF, which takes a set of exploits as input and returns a set of vulnerabilities (i.e. $ExF : \mathbf{Ex} \rightarrow 2^V$). The set of vulnerabilities produced by $ExF(A)$, for a given set of exploits A, represents the vulnerabilities that are exploited by the exploits in A. While many possible variations of an exploit function are possible, in this chapter, we will use a straightforward definition that extends the exploit function from singletons (whose associated vulnerabilities can be taken directly from the online marketplaces) to sets of exploits: $ExF(A) = \bigcup_{a \in A} ExF(\{a\})$. For use in proving complexity results, we shall denote the special case where $Ex = V$, $ExF(A) = A$, and $\forall ex \in Ex$, $c_{ex} = 1$ as the "Identity Exploit Model."

Player Strategies and Payoff. An attacker will use a set of exploits to attempt to gain access to a system, and must do so within a budget. Likewise, the defender must identify a set of vulnerabilities that he is willing to expose (often referred to as the "presented attack surface"). We define strategies for the two players formally as follows.

Definition 6.2.1 (*Attack Strategy*). *Given budget* $k_{atk} \in \mathbb{R}^+$, *an Attack Strategy, denoted A, is a subset of Ex s.t.* $\sum_{a \in A} c_a \leq k_{atk}$.

Definition 6.2.2 (*Defense Strategy*). *Given a family of application constraint sets* $\mathcal{C} = \{\mathcal{C}_0, \mathcal{C}_1, \ldots, \mathcal{C}_n\}$, *a Defense Strategy, denoted D, is a subset of V s.t. for each* $\mathcal{C}_i \in \mathcal{C}$, *there exists* $C \in \mathcal{C}_i$ *where* $C \subseteq D$.

Note that when a defense strategy D meets the requirements of $\mathcal{C}$, as per Definition 6.2.2, we say D *satisfies* $\mathcal{C}$. We will use the notation $\mathbf{A}, \mathbf{D}$ to denote the set of all attack and defense strategies, respectively, and refer to an attacker-defender pair of strategies as a "strategy profile." We will also define a *mixed strategy* for both players in the normal manner. For the attacker (resp. defender) a mixed strategy is a probability distribution over $\mathbf{A}$ (resp. $\mathbf{D}$). We shall normally denote mixed strategies as Pr_A, Pr_D for each player and use the notation $|Pr_A|$ (resp. $|Pr_D|$) to denote the number of strategies in $\mathbf{A}$ (resp. $\mathbf{D}$) that are assigned a nonzero probability by the mixed strategy. We now turn our attention to the payoff function, which we define formally as follows:

Definition 6.2.3 (*Payoff Function*). *A payoff function, p, is any function that takes a strategy profile as an argument and returns a positive real. Formally,*
$$p : A \times D \to \mathbb{R}^+$$

Unless noted otherwise, we will treat the payoff function as being computable in polynomial time. Also, the payoff function is under-specified—which is designed to allow flexibility in the framework. However, in the context of the results of this chapter, we shall consider the following "payoff function axioms":

$$\forall D \in \mathbf{D}, \forall A \in \mathbf{A} \text{ s.t. } ExF(A) \cap D = \emptyset, \ p(A, D) = 0 \qquad (6.1)$$

$$\forall D \in \mathbf{D}, \ \forall D' \subseteq D, \forall A \in \mathbf{A}, \ p(A, D') \leq p(A, D) \qquad (6.2)$$

$$\forall D \in \mathbf{D}, \ \forall A \in \mathbf{A}, \ \forall A' \subseteq A, \ p(A', D) \leq p(A, D) \qquad (6.3)$$

$$\forall A \in \mathbf{A}, \ D, D' \in \mathbf{D}, p(A, D) + p(A, D') \geq p(A, D \cup D') \qquad (6.4)$$

$$\forall D \in \mathbf{D}, \ A, A' \in \mathbf{A}, p(A, D) + p(A', D) \geq p(A \cup A', D). \qquad (6.5)$$

Axiom 6.1 states that if the vulnerabilities generated by an attack strategy's exploits and the vulnerabilities in a defense strategy are disjoint sets, the payoff function must return 0. A consequence of axiom 6.1 is that if either the attack strategy or the defense strategy is the empty set, the payoff function will return 0. Axioms 6.2 and 6.3 require the payoff function to be monotonic in the size of the attack and defense strategies. Axioms 6.4 and 6.5 require the payoff function to be submodular with respect to the attack and defense strategies.

Definition 6.2.4 *(Expected Payoff Function). Further, when dealing with mixed strategies, we shall discuss payoff in terms of expectation. Expected payoff can be formally defined as follows:*

$$Exp(Pr_A, Pr_D) = \sum_{D \in D} \sum_{A \in A} Pr_A(A) Pr_D(D) p(A, D).$$

Overlap Payoff Function Perhaps the simplest payoff function would be one that only considers how many vulnerabilities are in common between those that are exploited by the attack strategy and those present in the defense strategy. This payoff function can be described as $p(A, D) = \frac{|ExF(A) \cap D|}{|Z|}$, where $|Z|$ can be $|D|$, $|V|$, or simply 1.

In the case when $|Z| = 1$, and hence $p(A, D) = |ExF(A) \cap D|$, we can intuitively think of the payoff as simply the number of vulnerabilities exploited by the attacker. Using the overlap function, the expected payoff can be interpreted as the "expected number of exploited vulnerabilities."

Attacker Constraint Payoff Function Another possible payoff function may introduce weights to certain vulnerabilities, because perhaps certain vulnerabilities are more valuable to an attacker. For example, let $\mathcal{W}$ be a set of attacker weight constraint sets, where each attacker weight constraint set is defined $\mathcal{W}_i \subseteq 2^V$. Each attacker weight constraint can have an associated value, w_i, which represents the "value" of that specific set. An attack strategy A would satisfy $\mathcal{W}_i$ if $\exists W \in \mathcal{W}_i$ s.t. $W \subseteq ExF(A)$. This construction is analogous to the application constraint set construction for the defender.

Using $\mathcal{W}$ and the associated weights for each constraint set $\mathcal{W}_i \in \mathcal{W}$, the following payoff function can be constructed. Let $\mathcal{W}_{A,D}$ represent the set of attacker weight constraint sets that are satisfied by attack strategy A and also made available, or satisfied, by a defense strategy D. That is,

$$\mathcal{W}_{A,D} = \{\mathcal{W}_i \in \mathcal{W} | \exists W \in \mathcal{W}_i \text{ s.t. } W \subseteq ExF(A) \text{ and } W \subseteq D\}.$$

Using this, the payoff function is defined

$$p(A, D) = \frac{\sum_{\mathcal{W}_i \in \mathcal{W}_{A,D}} w_i}{\sum_{\mathcal{W}_i \in \mathcal{W}} w_i}.$$

This will generate a value in the range $[0, 1]$ and adheres to axiom 6.1, axiom 6.2, and axiom 6.3. This "Attacker Constraint Payoff Function" can be seen to generate the "Overlap Payoff Function" by the following construction:

$$\forall V_i \in V$$

$$\mathcal{W}_i = \{\{V_i\}\}$$

$$\text{and } w_i = 1.$$

6.2.1 Deterministic Problem Formulations

We now have the components to define a pair of decision problems dealing with the best response for the players. These problems are the deterministic host attacker problem (DHAP) and deterministic host defender problem (DHDP), respectively, and are defined as follows:

DHAP.
INPUT: $k_{atk} \in \mathbb{R}^+$, $x \in \mathbb{R}^+$, mixed defense strategy Pr_D, and payoff function p.
OUTPUT: "Yes" if $\exists A \in \mathbf{A}$ s.t. $\sum_{a \in A} c_a \leq k_{atk}$, and $\sum_{D \in \mathbf{D}} Pr_D(D) p(A, D) \geq x$, "No" otherwise.

DHDP.
INPUT: $x \in \mathbb{R}^+$, application constraints $\mathcal{C}$, mixed attack strategy Pr_A, and payoff function p.
OUTPUT: "Yes" if $\exists D \in \mathbf{D}$ s.t. $\sum_{A \in \mathbf{A}} Pr_A(A) p(A, D) \leq x$ and D satisfies $\mathcal{C}$ and "No" otherwise.

The natural optimization variants for these two problems will deal with maximizing the payoff in DHAP and minimizing the payoff in DHDP.

6.2.2 Nondeterministic Problem Formulations

By introducing nondeterminism, we are able to begin dealing with probability distributions over strategies. This adds a lot of flexibility with how a defender can configure multiple machines. That is, the best way to defend a given computer network might be to have different machines configured in different ways. With nondeterminism, we can capture concepts such as moving target defense (MTD) [48, 47], which aims to dynamically vary the attack surface that is presented to the attacker in order to make the discovery and exploitation of vulnerabilities more difficult, in our model.

Definition 6.2.5 *(Mixed Strategy Profile). A mixed strategy profile is a tuple consisting of a mixed attack strategy and a mixed defense strategy. For a given mixed attack strategy, Pr_A, and a given mixed defense strategy, Pr_D, the mixed strategy profile is denoted by (Pr_A, Pr_D).*

With a mixed strategy profile, we have a probabilistic distribution over strategies for both the attacker and the defender.

Definition 6.2.6 *(Minimax Strategy Profile). A mixed strategy profile, (Pr_A, Pr_D), is a minimax strategy profile if*

$$\nexists Pr'_A \in \mathbf{Pr_A} \; s.t. \; \forall Pr'_D \in \mathbf{Pr_D}, \; Exp(Pr'_A, Pr'_D) > Exp(Pr_A, Pr_D)$$

$$and \; \nexists Pr'_D \in \mathbf{Pr_D} \; s.t. \; \forall Pr'_A \in \mathbf{Pr_A}, \; Exp(Pr'_A, Pr'_D) < Exp(Pr_A, Pr_D).$$

Definition 6.2.7 *((η, θ) Minimax Strategy Profile). A mixed strategy profile, (Pr_A, Pr_D), is an (η, θ) minimax strategy profile if*

$$|Pr_A| \leq \eta \; and \; \nexists Pr'_A \in \mathbf{Pr_A} \; s.t. \; |Pr'_A| \leq \eta$$

$$and \; \forall Pr'_D \in \mathbf{Pr_D} \; Exp(Pr'_A, Pr'_D) > Exp(Pr_A, Pr_D)$$

$$and \; |Pr_D| \leq \theta \; and \; \nexists Pr'_D \in \mathbf{Pr_D} \; s.t. \; |Pr'_D| \leq \theta$$

$$and \; \forall Pr'_A \in \mathbf{Pr_A} \; Exp(Pr'_A, Pr'_D) < Exp(Pr_A, Pr_D).$$

As the number of possible deterministic attack and defense strategies grows exponentially with the size of the Ex and V, respectively, it is useful to introduce a size constraint to the number of strategies that can receive a nonzero probability. This is precisely what an (η, θ) Minimax Strategy Profile is; we are limiting the number of attack and defense strategies that receive nonzero probabilities to η and θ, respectively.

6.2.2.1 Minimax Problem

INPUT: $k_{atk}, \mathcal{C}, p, V$

OUTPUT: (Pr_A, Pr_D), where (Pr_A, Pr_D) is a minimax strategy profile with respect to the payoff function, p, such that all $A \in \{A | Pr_A(A) > 0\}$, $D \in \{D | Pr_D(D) > 0\}$ adhere to the constraints represented by k_{atk} and $\mathcal{C}$, respectively.

6.2.2.2 (η, θ) Minimax Problem

INPUT: $k_{atk}, \mathcal{C}, p, V, \eta, \theta$

OUTPUT: (Pr_A, Pr_D), where (Pr_A, Pr_D) is an (η, θ) minimax strategy profile with respect to the payoff function, p, such that all $A \in \{A | Pr_A(A) > 0\}$, $D \in \{D | Pr_D(D) > 0\}$ adhere to the constraints represented by k_{atk} and $\mathcal{C}$, respectively.

6.2.2.3 Mixed Defense Strategy

Consider a network which consists of an arbitrary number of systems. Let V represent the universe of possible vulnerabilities that an attacker would attempt to exploit. Additionally, let $\mathcal{V}$ be a vector of size $|V|$ such that the ith component in $\mathcal{V}$ (denoted v_i) represents the fraction of systems that have vulnerability i in their presented attack surface (e.g., $v_i = 1$ if $i \in D$ for all systems). If t is the number of systems probed by an attacker, then one possible mixed defense strategy is

$$Pr_D(D) = \prod_{i \in D}((1 - v_i)^t) \times \prod_{i \notin D}(1 - (1 - v_i)^t)$$

Here, $Pr_D(D)$ is the probability that given a a set of t systems picked at random, all of them will have a presented attack surface consisting of exactly the vulnerabilities in D. Note that this mixed strategy distribution assumes independence between systems as well as vulnerabilities.

6.3 Computational Complexity

With the model and problems formally defined, we can begin to analyze the complexity of the problems, determining computational class membership as well as polynomial time approximation bounds for each of them (Tables 6.2, 6.3 and 6.4). All proofs use the "Identity Exploit Model" for attack strategies, unless otherwise specified.

Table 6.2. *Summary of complexity results*

Opp. Strat.	Attacker	Defender
Det.	PTIME when $k_{atk} \geq |D|$ (Prop. 6.3.4), NP-Complete in general (Thm. 2)	PTIME when $|\mathcal{C}| = 1$ (Prop. 6.3.1), NP-Complete in general (Thm. 1)
Mixed	PTIME when $k_{atk} = 1$ (Prop. 6.3.3), NP-Complete in general (Thm. 2)	PTIME when $|\mathcal{C}| = 1$ (Prop. 6.3.2), NP-Complete in general (Thm. 1)

6.3.1 Deterministic Host Defender Problem (DHDP)

Proposition 6.3.1 *When $|Pr_A| = 1$ and $|\mathcal{C}| = 1$, DHDP is solvable in polynomial time when the payoff function adheres to the monotonicity axioms.*

Proof Let A be the lone attack strategy with nonzero probability and $\mathcal{C}_1$ be the lone application constraint set. The optimal defense strategy, in this case, is equal to the constraint set, C_i, in $\mathcal{C}_1$ which minimizes the payoff function. This is a consequence of the monotonicity constraint of the payoff function. It then follows that the minimum value of the payoff function is simply

$$\min_{C \in \mathcal{C}_1} p(A, C).$$

This value can be computed in polynomial time with respect to $|\mathcal{C}_1|$. Once the payoff function is minimized, it can be compared to the parameter x and the corresponding result can be returned. □

Theorem 1 *When $|\mathcal{C}| > 1$ and $|Pr_A| = 1$, DHDP is NP-Complete.*

Claim 1 *DHDP is in the class NP under the specified constraints.*

Proof Let A be the lone attack strategy with a nonzero probability. Clearly, a defense strategy, D, can be verified to adhere to the output constraints of DHDP in polynomial time by simply computing $p(A, D)$ and comparing the result with x. This ability to verify a given defense strategy in polynomial time implies membership in the class NP. □

Table 6.3. *Summary of approximation limits*

Problem	Approximation limit
DHDP	$(1 - o(1))ln(n)$ (Thm. 3)
DHAP	$\left(1 - \frac{1}{e}\right)$ (Thm. 4)

Table 6.4. *Summary of minimax problem
complexity results*

Problem	Complexity result
Minimax problem	NP-Hard (Thm. 5)
(η, θ) Minimax problem	NP-Hard (Thm. 6)

Claim 2 *"Hitting Set" can be embedded into DHDP in polynomial time under
these constraints.*

Proof Hitting set is a well-known NP-Hard problem that is defined as follows.
As input, Hitting Set takes a finite set S, a collection of subsets of S, denoted
B, and a natural number $K \leq |S|$. Hitting Set then returns "Yes" if there exists
$S' \subseteq S$ such that $|S'| \leq K$ and S' contains at least one element from each subset
of B, and "No" otherwise. To embed Hitting Set into DHDP, using the Identity
Exploit Model , let $V = A = S$, $x = \frac{K}{|V|}$, and $p(A, D) = \frac{|D \cap A|}{|V|}$. To construct C,
let there be an application constraint set, C_i for each B_i in B. Each application
constraint set will then be $C_i = \{\{b_i\}|b_i \in B_i\}$. Application constraint set C_i is
made up of singleton sets for each element in B_i. Note that constructing C takes
only polynomial time. $\qquad\square$

Claim 3 *A "Yes" from DHDP implies a "Yes" from Hitting Set.*

Proof By way of contradiction, suppose there is a "Yes" answer to the instance
of DHDP and a "No" answer to Hitting Set. A "Yes" answer to DHDP implies
that a defense strategy was found such that the payoff function yielded a result
less than or equal to x. This conclusion implies the following result,

$$p(A, D) \leq x$$

$$p(A, D) = \frac{|D \cap A|}{|V|}, \quad x = \frac{K}{|V|}$$

$$\frac{|D \cap A|}{|V|} \leq \frac{K}{|V|}.$$

As $A = V$, $D \subseteq V$, we must have that D is a subset of A and that the intersection of A and D is simply D. By the definition of the overlap payoff function and
the chosen value of x, namely $\frac{K}{|V|}$, we can conclude that $|D| \leq K$. Additionally,
a "Yes" in DHDP implies that a D was found that satisfies the application constraints, which implies that at least one element from each subset of B appears
in D. Since at least one element from each subset of B appears in D, a "No"

from Hitting Set implies that $|D| > K$ this is a contradiction to the result from DHDP. □

Claim 4 *A "No" from DHDP implies a "No" from Hitting Set.*

Proof Suppose, by way of contradiction, there is a "No" answer to DHDP and a "Yes" answer to "Hitting Set." A "Yes" to Hitting Set implies that $\exists D \subseteq V$ s.t. $|D| \leq K$ where D contains at least one element from every subset in B. Let $\mathbf{D}$ be the set of all possible defense sets that satisfy the application constraints (i.e., contain at least one element from each set in B). A "No" to DHDP then implies the following,

$$\forall D \in \mathbf{D},$$

$$p(A, D) > x$$

$$\frac{|D \cap A|}{|V|} > \frac{K}{|V|}$$

$$|D| > |K|.$$

This is a contradiction. □

Proof of Theorem 1 By claims 1-4, DHDP is NP-Complete when $|\mathcal{C}| > 1$. □

Proposition 6.3.2 *When $|Pr_A| > 1$ and $|\mathcal{C}| = 1$, DHDP is solvable in polynomial time (w.r.t $|Pr_A|$) when the payoff function adheres to the monotonicity axioms.*

Proof Let $\mathcal{C}_1$ denote the lone application constraint set. The defense strategy that will produce the the minimum value of the payoff function is simply the constraint set, C_i, in $\mathcal{C}_1$ such that C_i minimizes the expected payoff. The lowest expected payoff is then given as

$$\min_{C_i \in \mathcal{C}_1} \sum_{A|Pr_A(A)>0} Pr_A(A)p(A, C_i).$$

This value can be computed in polynomial time with respect to $|\mathcal{C}_1|$ and $|Pr_A|$. Once the minimum expected payoff has been computed, it can be compared to the parameter x and the appropriate result can be returned. □

6.3.2 Deterministic Host Attacker Problem (DHAP)

Proposition 6.3.3 *Under the Identity Exploit Model, when $k_{atk} = 1$, even when $|Pr_D| > 1$, DHAP can be solved in polynomial time (w.r.t. $|Ex|$).*

Proof Under the "Identity Exploit Model," $k_{atk} = 1$ implies that the attack strategy can consist of only a single exploit. Therefore, the optimal attack strategy will then be the single exploit that maximizes the expected payoff. The maximum payoff can simply computed as follows,

$$\max_{ex \in Ex} \sum_{D|Pr_D(D)>0} Pr_D(D)p((ex), D).$$

This maximum payoff is seen to be computable in polynomial time with respect to the total number of exploits, $|Ex|$, and the set of all defense strategies with nonzero probabilities. After computing the maximum payoff, it can be compared with the input value x in constant time, and the appropriate result can be returned. □

Proposition 6.3.4 *When $|Pr_D| = 1$ and $k_{atk} \geq |D|$, where D is the lone defense strategy with a nonzero probability, DHAP can be solved in polynomial time under the Identity Exploit Model.*

Proof Under the "Identity Exploit Model," if k_{atk} is greater than the size of the lone defense strategy, the Attacker can simply choose an attack strategy that contains every vulnerability in the defense strategy. As seen in the payoff function axioms, if the attack and defense strategies are equal, the payoff function has a value of 1. When the payoff function returns 1, the result of DHAP is always "Yes." □

Theorem 2 *DHAP is NP-Complete, even when $|Pr_D| = 1$ and the payoff function adheres to the submodularity and monotonicity axioms.*

Claim 1 *DHAP is in the class NP.*

Proof As the payoff function can be computed in polynomial time, it is clear that a certificate of DHAP can be verified to adhere to the output constraints in polynomial time. Because of this, DHAP is in the class NP. □

Claim 2 *"Hitting Set" can be embedded into an instance of DHAP in polynomial time.*

Proof Let D denote the lone defense strategy with a nonzero probability in mixed strategy Pr_D, i.e., $Pr_D(D) = 1$. Again, as input, Hitting Set takes a finite set S, a collection of subsets of S, denoted B, and a natural number $K \leq |S|$. The output of Hitting Set is "Yes" if there exist $S' \subseteq S$ such that $|S'| \leq K$ and S' contains an element from every subset in B, and "No" otherwise.

To embed Hitting Set into DHAP using the Identity Exploit Model, let $V = D = S$, $x = 1$, $k_{atk} = K$, and the payoff function be set to the Attacker

Constraint Payoff Function from Section 6.2 such that a Weight Constraint Set $\mathcal{W}_i$ is defined for each subset $B_i \in B$ as $\mathcal{W}_i = \{\{b_i\}|b_i \in B_i\}$ with corresponding weight $w_i = 1$. As mentioned in Section 6.2, the payoff function above can be seen to adhere to the monotonicity and submodularity axioms. The Attacker Constraint Payoff Function only returns a value of 1 if every weight constraint set, $\mathcal{W}_i$, is satisfied by both the attack and defense strategies. The defense strategy is equal to the set of all vulnerabilities, V, and hence will automatically satisfy all Weight Constraint Sets. Thus, it can be seen that in order for an attack strategy to satisfy all Weight Constraint Sets, and in turn produce a payoff of 1, at least one element from each subset of B must be present in the attack strategy. It is clear that this embedding can be performed in polynomial time.   □

Claim 3 *A "Yes" from DHAP implies a "Yes" for Hitting Set.*

Proof Suppose, by way of contradiction, that Hitting Set returns "No" and DHAP returns "Yes." A "No" from Hitting Set implies that there does not exist $S' \subseteq S$ such that S' contains an element from each subset in B and $|S'| \leq K$. A "Yes" from DHAP implies that

$$\exists A \subseteq V \text{ s.t. } |A| \leq k_{atk} \text{ and } p(A, D) \geq x.$$

Since $x = 1$, this implies that the payoff must be 1. As stated previously, a payoff of 1 implies that the both A and D contain at least one element from each set in B. Additionally, a "Yes" from DHAP implies that there exists an A such that A adheres to the size constraint (i.e. $|A| \leq k_{atk}$) while simultaneously producing a payoff of 1. Consequently, this DHAP result implies that there must exist an A which is a subset of S and contains one element from each set in B such that $|A| \leq k_{atk} = K$. This is a contradiction with the Hitting Set result.   □

Claim 4 *A "No" from DHAP implies a "No" from Hitting Set*

Proof Suppose, by way of contradiction, that Hitting Set returns "Yes" and DHAP returns "No." A "Yes" from Hitting Set implies that there exists $S' \subseteq S$ such that S' contains at least one element from each set in B and $|S'| \leq K$. A "No" from DHAP implies that there does not exist $A \subseteq V = S$ such that $p(A, D) = 1$ and $|A| \leq k_{atk} = K$. This is a contradiction since a "No" from DHAP implies that no subset of S satisfies the size constraint ($|A| \leq k_{atk}$) and contains at least one element from each set in B ($p(A, D) = 1$).   □

Proof of Theorem 2 By claims 1–4, DHAP is NP-Complete when $|Pr_D| = 1$ and the payoff function adheres to the submodularity and monotonicity axioms.   □

These reductions to Hitting Set for DHAP and DHDP have immediate consequences regarding limits of approximation for the optimization forms of both DHAP and DHDP. As the Hitting Set problem is equivalent to the Set Cover problem, the approximation bounds for Set Cover also apply to Hitting Set.

Theorem 3 *DHDP can not be approximated where the payoff is within a factor of $(1 - o(1))ln(n)$ unless $P = NP$.*

Proof The results from [34] state that it is NP-Hard to approximate Set Cover below the threshold $(1 - o(1))ln(n)$, where n is the size of the cover. As seen in Theorem 1, the defense strategy that satisfies the output constraints of DHDP is also the set which satisfies the Hitting Set constraints. In fact, an optimal defense strategy produced from the embedding in Theorem 1 is also an optimal solution to Hitting Set. In DHDP, an optimal defense strategy is a defense strategy of minimal size that satisfies all of the application constraints. This is analogous to Hitting Set in that an optimal solution of Hitting Set is a set of minimal size while still containing an element from each of the subsets in B (see Theorem 1 for problem definition). The constant-factor reduction requirement to maintain an approximation bound is clearly met. Thus, the optimization version of DHDP shares the approximation bound with Hitting Set and Set Cover, namely a $(1 - o(1))ln(n)$ threshold within which approximation becomes NP-Hard. □

Theorem 4 *DHAP can not be approximated where the payoff is within a factor of $(1 - \frac{1}{e})$ unless $P = NP$.*

Proof The results from [34] prove that it is NP-Hard to approximate max k-cover within a threshold of $(1 - \frac{1}{e})$. Theorem 2 shows that Hitting Set (which is equivalent to Set Cover) can be embedded into DHAP. For the optimization version of DHAP, a set of size less than or equal to k_{atk} that maximizes the number of satisfied Weight Constraint Sets is returned. This is analogous to the optimization version of max k-cover, which returns a set S of size less than or equal to some constant k, such that S maximizes the number of subsets in B "covered" (or "hit"). An optimal result of the optimization version of DHAP is indeed an optimal result of the Hitting Set version of max k-cover. This constant factor correspondence between max-k cover and DHAP implies that the approximation bound is the same for both problems and that it is NP-Hard to approximate DHAP within a threshold of $(1 - \frac{1}{e})$. □

Theorem 5 *The Minimax Problem is NP-Hard.*

    To produce a predictable defense strategy, we will fix the application constraints with $C = \{\{V\}\}$. By doing this, the only valid defense strategy is equal *to the set of all vulnerabilities (i.e., $D = V$) and any mixed defense strategy profile that is produced must adhere to the constraint $Pr_D(V) = 1$.*

Claim 1 *For a minimax strategy profile, (Pr_A, Pr_D), when $|Pr_D| = 1$, every strategy in Pr_A produces the same payoff.*

Proof Let (Pr_A, Pr_D) be a minimax strategy profile such that $D \in Pr_D$ and $Pr_D(D) = 1$. Let $A', A'' \in Pr_A$ be two deterministic attack strategies such that $p(A', D) \leq p(A'', D)$. It follows that $Pr_A(A')p(A', D) + Pr_A(A'')p(A'', D) \leq (Pr_A(A') + Pr_A(A''))p(A'', D)$. That is, the expected payoff,

$$Exp(Pr_A, Pr_D) = \sum_{A \in Pr_A, D \in Pr_D} Pr_A(A)p(A, D)$$

will be maximized when all strategies in Pr_A are best responses to D and hence produce the same (maximum) payoff. □

Claim 2 *The solution of the Minimax Problem can be used to solve an instance of DHAP.*

Proof Let (Pr_A, Pr_D) be the solution to the Minimax Problem where V, p, and k_{atk} are arbitrary values and $C = \{\{V\}\}$. By fixing the application constraints, we know that $Pr_D(V) = 1$. By claim 1, we know that $\forall A \in Pr_A$ s.t. $Pr_A > 0$, $p(A, V) = c$, where c is a constant in the range $[0, 1]$ that represents the maximum payoff.

To solve DHAP, take any $A \in Pr_A$ such that $Pr_A(A) > 0$, compare $p(A, V)$ with the input parameter x, and return the corresponding result. Theorem 2 states that solving DHAP when $|Pr_D| = 1$, and more specifically when $Pr_D(V) = 1$, is NP-Hard. Therefore, the Minimax Problem must be NP-Hard, as a polynomial time solution to the Minimax Problem would imply that the instance of DHAP presented in Theorem 2, and consequently the Hitting Set problem, have polynomial time solutions. □

Proof of Theorem 5 By claims 1–3, the Minimax Problem is NP-Hard. □

Theorem 6 *The (η, θ) Minimax Problem is NP-Hard, even when $\eta = 1$ and $\theta = 1$.*

Proof Using the same construction used in Theorem 5 (i.e., $C = \{\{V\}\}$) and setting $\eta = \theta = 1$, Pr_D will be produced such that $Pr_D(V) = 1$. By the same argument in Theorem 5 the attack strategy with nonzero probability in the mixed attack strategy is the solution to optimization version of DHAP. That is, A s.t. $Pr_A(A) = 1$ maximizes $p(A, V)$. If the (η, θ) Minimax Problem could be solved in polynomial time, then DHAP could be solved in polynomial time by simply comparing $p(A, V)$ with x. This contradicts Theorem 2. $\qquad\square$

Theorem 7 *When the payoff function adheres to axioms 6.1, 6.3, and 6.5, a greedy approximation algorithm for DHAP provides the best polynomial time approximation, unless P=NP.*

Claim 1 *Greedy approximation provides a $(1 - \frac{1}{e})$ approximation bound to DHAP when the defense strategy is fixed.*

Proof Let $p_D(A)$ represent the payoff function for a fixed defense strategy (i.e. $p_D(A) = p(A, D)$ when D is held constant). The results from [78] show that greedy approximation algorithms provide a $(1 - \frac{1}{e})$-approximation for normalized monotone submodular functions. By adhering to axioms 6.1, 6.3, and 6.5, the payoff function, $p_D(A)$, is a normalized monotone submodular function, and hence a greedy approximation will provide a $(1 - \frac{1}{e})$-approximation bound for DHAP. $\qquad\square$

Proof of Theorem 7 Theorem 4 showed that $(1 - \frac{1}{e})$ is the polynomial-time approximation bound, unless P=NP, of DHAP. Claim 1 in Theorem 7 shows that greedy approximation provides a $(1 - \frac{1}{e})$ approximation for DHAP when the payoff function is normalized, monotonic, and submodular. Thus, a greedy approximation algorithm provides the best possible polynomial-time approximation, namely $(1 - \frac{1}{e})$ within an optimal solution, for DHAP. $\qquad\square$

6.4 Algorithms

As our complexity results show, in the general case, finding optimal solutions for the problems presented in this chapter are NP-Hard, and thus intractable. To deal with this intractability, this section presents polynomial-time approximation algorithms to provide approximate solutions to the problems.

Summary of DHAP algorithms

Algorithm description	Approx. bound	Assumptions	Citation
Lazy greedy	$\frac{1}{2}(1 - 1/e)$	p is submod.	[76]
Mult. update	$(1 - \epsilon)(1 - 1/e)$	p is submod.	[6]

Summary of DHDP algorithms

Algorithm description	Approx. bound	Assumptions	Citation
Weighted set cover	$(ln(n) + 1)$	p is overlap $|C| = 1$	[27]
Greedy hitting set	$(ln(n) + 1)$	p is modular. $|C| = 1$	[76]

Definition 6.4.1 *(Marginal Gain). Given a payoff function p and a mixed defense strategy Pr_D, $\Delta_{p,Pr_D}(a|A)$ will measure the marginal gain of exploit a in the context of an attack strategy A. That is,*

$$\Delta_{p,Pr_D}(a|A) = \sum_{D \in Pr_D} p(A \cup \{a\}, D) - p(A, D).$$

With the limits of approximation in mind, we can now introduce several algorithms to solve the optimization variants of DHAP and DHDP. The optimization variant of DHAP under the overlap payoff function is a special case of submodular maximization with the distinction that we are not simply picking k discrete objects, but instead picking items that each have a unique cost associated with them. Understanding this, we examine several different approaches to this problem based on the literature on submodular maximization. DHDP, on the other hand, can be readily approximated using the traditional set-cover algorithm (under some realistic assumptions), as cost does not affect DHDP.

6.4.1 Algorithms for DHAP

Greedy Approaches. As mentioned earlier, the non-unit cost of exploits mean that DHAP can be considered as a submodular maximization problem subject to knapsack constraints. Two versions of the traditional greedy algorithm [78] can be applied: a cost-benefit variant and uniform-cost variant, both of which will also use the lazy-greedy optimization [76] to further enhance performance while maintaining the approximation guarantee. We note that independently, the uniform-cost and the cost-benefit algorithms can perform arbitrarily badly. However, by extending a result from [61], either the cost-benefit or the uniform-cost algorithm will provide a solution within a factor of $\frac{1}{2}(1 - 1/e)$ for a given set of input parameters. By applying both algorithms to a given problem instance and returning the attack strategy which produces the larger payoff, the $\frac{1}{2}(1 - 1/e)$ approximation factor is achieved for DHAP. A cost-benefit

---

Algorithm 1 Lazy Greedy algorithm (cost-benefit variant)

Input: $k_{atk} \in \mathbb{R}^+$, Pr_D, and payoff function p.
Output: $A \subseteq Ex$ s.t. $\sum_{a \in A} c_a \leq k_{atk}$

1: $A \leftarrow \emptyset$; $cost \leftarrow 0$; priority queue $Q \leftarrow \emptyset$; $iter \leftarrow 1$
2: **for** $e \in Ex$ **do**
3:     $e.key \leftarrow \frac{\Delta_{p,Pr_D}(e|\emptyset)}{c_e}$; $e.i \leftarrow 1$
4:     insert e into Q with "key" as the key
5: **while** $\{a \in Ex \backslash A : c_a + cost \leq k_{atk}\} \neq \emptyset$ **do**
6:     extract top (max) element e of Q
7:     **if** $e.i = iter$ and $c_e + cost \leq k_{atk}$ **then**
8:         $A \leftarrow A \cup \{e\}$; $iter \leftarrow iter + 1$
9:         $cost \leftarrow cost + c_e$
10:    **else if** $c_e + cost \leq k_{atk}$ **then**
11:        $e.i \leftarrow iter$; $e.key \leftarrow \frac{\Delta_{p,Pr_D}(e|A)}{c_e}$;
12:        re-insert e into Q
13: **return** A

---

lazy approximation algorithm is shown in Algorithm 1. By removing "c_e" from the denominator in the $e.key$ assignment in lines 3 and 11, the cost-benefit lazy approximation algorithm is transformed into a uniform cost lazy approximation algorithm.

Multiplicative Update Approach. An improved approximation ratio, when compared with the $\frac{1}{2}(1 - 1/e)$ ratio for the greedy algorithms, can be obtained by adapting Algorithm 1 from [6] for DHAP. This is shown as Algorithm 2 in this chapter. For some value ϵ (a parameter), this algorithm provides a $(1 - \epsilon)(1 - 1/e)$ approximation of the optimal solution (Theorem 1.2 in [6]), which, by providing an exceedingly small ϵ value, can get arbitrarily close to the $(1 - 1/e)$ optimal approximation limit we discussed earlier.

6.4.1.1 Algorithms for DHDP

When using the overlap payoff function, DHDP can be modeled as a weighted set cover problem. Because the overlap payoff function is a modular function, the associated cost of a given vulnerability v, is simply the payoff produced by the singleton set $\{v\}$ with a mixed attack strategy Pr_A (i.e., $c_v = \sum_{A \in Pr_A} Pr_A(A)p(A, \{v\})$. In the common case where each constraint set is a singleton set (i.e., $\forall C_i \in \mathcal{C}$, $\forall C \in \mathcal{C}_i$, $|C| = 1$), if the overlap payoff function is used, an adaptation on the standard greedy weighted set cover algorithm can be used for DHDP (Algorithm 3), providing a $ln(n) + 1$ approximation [34].

Algorithm 2 Multiplicative Update

Input: $k_{atk}, \epsilon \in \mathbb{R}^+$ s.t. $0 < \epsilon \leq 1$, Pr_D, and payoff function p.

Output: $A \subseteq Ex$ s.t. $\sum_{a \in A} c_a \leq k_{atk}$

1: $Ex' \leftarrow \{ex \in Ex : c_{ex} \leq k_{atk}\}$

2: $A \leftarrow \emptyset$

3: $W \leftarrow \min_{ex'_i \in |Ex'|} k_{atk}^2 / c_{ex'_i}$

4: $w \leftarrow 1/k_{atk}$; $\lambda \leftarrow e^{\epsilon W/4}$

5: **while** $k_{atk}w \leq \lambda$ and $Ex' \neq \emptyset$ **do**

6: $\quad ex_j \leftarrow \text{argmin}_{ex_j \in Ex' \backslash A} \frac{c_{ex_j}}{k_{atk}} w / \Delta_{p, Pr_D}(ex_j | A)$

7: $\quad A \leftarrow A \cup \{ex_j\}$

8: $\quad w \leftarrow w \lambda^{c_{ex_j}/k_{atk}^2}$

9: $\quad Ex' \leftarrow Ex' \backslash \{ex_j\}$

10: **if** $\sum_{A_i \in A} c_{A_i} \leq k_{atk}$ **then**

11: $\quad$ return A

12: **else if** $\sum_{D \in Pr_D} Pr_D(D) p(A \backslash \{ex_j\}, D) \geq$

13: $\sum_{D \in Pr_D} Pr_D(D) p(\{ex_j\}, D)$ **then**

14: $\quad$ return $A \backslash \{ex_j\}$

15: **else**

16: $\quad$ return $\{ex_j\}$

Further, instead of transforming the Hitting Set problem into Set Cover problem and using the standard Greedy Weighted Set Cover algorithm, as seen in Algorithm 3, we can simply use a lazy weighted Hitting Set algorithm, which is shown in Algorithm 4.

Algorithm 3 Weighted Greedy DHDP algorithm for Singleton Constraint Set and Overlap Payoff Function Case

---

Input: Vulnerabilities V, Pr_A, and application constraints $\mathcal{C}$.

Output: $D \subseteq V$ s.t. the application constraints $\mathcal{C}$ are satisfied.

1: $D \leftarrow \emptyset$

2: $S \leftarrow$ set s.t. $S_i = \{j : V_i \in \mathcal{C}_j$ where (V_i) is ith vulnerability in V $\}$

3: $c_{S_i} \leftarrow \sum_{A \in Pr_A} Pr_A(A) |ExF(A) \cap \{V_i\}|$

4: $\mathcal{C}' \leftarrow [|\mathcal{C}|]$

5: **while** $\mathcal{C}' \neq \emptyset$ **do**

6: $\quad S_i \leftarrow \text{argmax}_{S_i \in S} \frac{|S_i \cap \mathcal{C}'|}{c_{S_i}}$

7: $\quad \mathcal{C}' \leftarrow \mathcal{C}' \backslash S_i$

8: $\quad D \leftarrow D \cup \{V_i\}$

9: return D

Algorithm 4 Weighted Greedy Hitting Set with Lazy Evaluation for Modular Payoff Function and Singleton Constraint Set

---

Input: Vulnerabilities V, Pr_A, modular payoff function p, and application constraints C.

Output: $D \subseteq V$ s.t. the application constraints C are satisfied.

1: $D \leftarrow \emptyset$; $c_{V_i} \leftarrow \sum_{A \in Pr_A} Pr_A(A) p(A, \{V_i\})$
2: priority queue $Q \leftarrow \emptyset$; $iteration \leftarrow 1$
3: **for** $V_i \in V$ **do**
4:      $V_i.key \leftarrow \frac{|\{C_i \in C : V_i \in C_i\}|}{c_{V_i}}$; $V_i.it \leftarrow 1$
5:      insert V_i into Q with "key" as the key
6: **while** $C \neq \emptyset$ **do**
7:      extract top (max) element V_i of Q
8:      **if** $V_i.it = iteration$ **then**
9:          $D \leftarrow D \cup \{V_i\}$; $V \leftarrow V \backslash \{V_i\}$
10:         $iteration \leftarrow iteration + 1$
11:         $C \leftarrow C \backslash \{C_i \in C : \{V_i\} \in C_i\}$
12:      **else**
13:         $V_i.it \leftarrow iteration$
14:         $V_i.key \leftarrow \frac{|\{C_i \in C : V_i \in C_i\}|}{c_{V_i}}$
15:         reinsert V_i into Q
16: **return** D

Proposition 6.4.1 *Algorithm 4 has the same approximation ratio as Algorithm 3, the greedy set cover algorithm.*

Claim 2 *Algorithm 4 is equivalent to Algorithm 3, when Algorithm 4 uses the overlap payoff function.*

Proof In both Algorithm 4 and Algorithm 3, when an element V_i is added to D, V_i is the element that satisfies $V_i = \text{argmax}_{V_i \in V} \frac{|\{C_i \in C : \{V_i\} \in C_i\}|}{c_{V_i}}$. □

Proof Proof of Proposition 6.4.1 When selecting a vulnerability to add to D at each iteration, both Algorithm 3 and Algorithm 4 follow an identical process, therefore Algorithm 4 must have the same approximation ratio as Algorithm 3. □

6.4.1.2 Algorithms for Minimax Problem

To solve the Minimax Problem, we adapt the double-oracle algorithm presented in [73] which, given oracles for the deterministic problems, was shown to provide an optimal minimax profile. The linear programs we will use in the double-oracle framework are denoted DefLP and AtkLP for the defender and attacker,

---

Algorithm 5 Double Oracle for Host Defense Framework

 1: Initialize **D** and **A** with as singleton sets of arbitrary defense and attack strategies, respectively.
 2: **repeat**
 3:    $Pr_D^* \leftarrow \text{DefLP}(\mathbf{A}, \mathbf{D})$
 4:    $Pr_A^* \leftarrow \text{AtkLP}(\mathbf{A}, \mathbf{D})$
 5:    $D' \leftarrow DO(Pr_A^*)$
 6:    $A' \leftarrow AO(Pr_D^*)$
 7:    $\mathbf{D} \leftarrow \mathbf{D} \cup (D')$
 8:    $\mathbf{A} \leftarrow \mathbf{A} \cup (A')$
 9: **until** convergence
10: **return** (Pr_A^*, Pr_D^*)

---

respectively. Our adapted double-oracle algorithm is shown in Algorithm 5. Of course, we have already shown that the deterministic problems themselves are NP-Hard, so our approximation algorithms for DHAP and DHDP will have to suffice as oracles for the attacker and defender.

Definition 6.4.2 (*DefLP*). *Given a set of attack strategies* **A** *and a set of defense strategies* **D**, *DefLP is defined as:*

$$\min_{p^*, Pr_D^*} p^*$$

$$s.t. \quad p^* \geq \sum_{D \in \mathbf{D}} Pr_D^*(D) p(A, D) \quad \forall A \in \mathbf{A}$$

$$\sum_{D \in \mathbf{D}} Pr_D^*(D) = 1$$

$$Pr_D^*(D) \geq 0 \quad \forall D \in \mathbf{D}.$$

Definition 6.4.3 (*AtkLP*). *Given a set of attack strategies* **A** *and a set of defense strategies* **D**, *AtkLP is defined as:*

$$\max_{p^*, Pr_A^*} p^*$$

$$s.t. \quad p^* \leq \sum_{A \in \mathbf{A}} Pr_A^*(A) p(A, D) \quad \forall D \in \mathbf{D}$$

$$\sum_{A \in \mathbf{A}} Pr_A^*(A) = 1$$

$$Pr_A^*(A) \geq 0 \quad \forall A \in \mathbf{A}.$$

Proposition 6.4.2 *Algorithm 5 provides the optimal solution, given oracles that solve the deterministic problems optimally.*

Table 6.5. *Examples of exploits from darknet markets*

Prod.	Vuln.	Target	USD
Kernel Panic	X-display system	Linux $<=$ 3.13.0–48	$471.56
IE $<=$ 11	memory corr.	IE on Windows $<=$ 7	$35.00
RemoteShell	wpconfig.php	Wordpress MU	$1,500.00
0day RCE	WebView memory corr.	Android 4.1, 4.2	$36.50
WindowsLPE	win32k elev. of priv.	Windows $<=$ 8.1	$12.00–48.17
MS15-034 RCE	http.sys	Windows $<=$ 8.1	$311.97
FUD Flash Exp.	unspec.	FlashPlayer $<=$ 16.0.0.287	$600.00

Proof Theorem 1 in [73] shows that this double-oracle framework converges to a minimax solution, which is an optimal solution for this problem. □

6.5 Evaluation and Discussion

6.5.1 Evaluation Dataset

These experiments use data from the month of May 2015 from eight darknet marketplaces. The product list is comprised of 235 hacking tools, 167 of which were distinct. The products targeted 21 specific platforms, such as different versions of Adobe Flash, Linux, Microsoft Windows, and OS X, as well as online presences such as Facebook, Wordpress, and others. Hardware-related software, such as those associated with Point-of-Sale machines, routers, and servers, are also reflected in this number. Figure 6.2 illustrates the variety of products in the markets and Table 6.5 illustrates exemplar exploits.

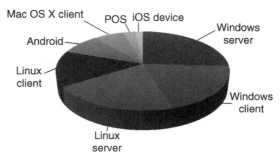

Figure 6.2. Distribution of exploits with respect to platform for the dataset used in this chapter.

6.5.2 System Configurations

As noted in Figure 6.2, a variety of platforms were represented in the dark-net market data used for this model. In this chapter, we describe results when using application constraints based on common configurations for Windows and Linux servers—as these were the most prominent targets of exploits found in this dataset. In our experiments, we mapped software such as media play-ers, databases, and FTP server software to application constraint sets to model the functional requirements of a system. We have also created (and conducted experiments with) models for Android, Point-of-Sale, and Apple systems—though qualitatively the results differed little from the Windows and Linux Server experiments.

6.5.3 DHAP Results

We implemented both the greedy and multiplicative update approaches to the DHAP problem. For the greedy algorithm, we studied three variants of greedy (cost-benefit, uniform cost, and a combination of the two) while we varied the parameter ϵ for the multiplicative update approach. We examined attacker pay-off as a function of budget (in Bitcoin). Figure 6.3 displays this result. Though the cost-benefit greedy algorithm has the potential to perform poorly, it was, in general, the best performing approach—despite the multiplicative update approach achieving the better approximation guarantee. Further, the multiplica-tive update algorithm (Algorithm 2) was consistently the slowest in terms of runtime, taking much longer than the lazy greedy algorithms, particularly for high values of k_{atk}. Despite the multiplicative update algorithm having a better theoretical approximation ratio when compared to the tandem of greedy algo-rithms, namely $(1 - \epsilon)(1 - 1/e)$ compared to $\frac{1}{2}(1 - 1/e)$, we see in Figure 6.3 that the greedy algorithms performed as well as or better than the multiplica-tive update very consistently. In all algorithms, as expected, runtime grew with budget (not pictured)—though the relationship was not strict, as an increase in budget does not necessarily mean that more exploits will be selected. In our experiments (on a commodity computer equipped with a 3.49 GHz i7 CPU and 16 GB of memory), our runtimes never exceeded ten minutes.

6.5.4 DHDP Results

Figure 6.4 demonstrate a defender's best response to an attack strategy against a Windows server and Linux server, respectively, for varying values of k_{atk}. Though we see similar trends in Figure 6.3 as we do in Figure 6.4, we see that

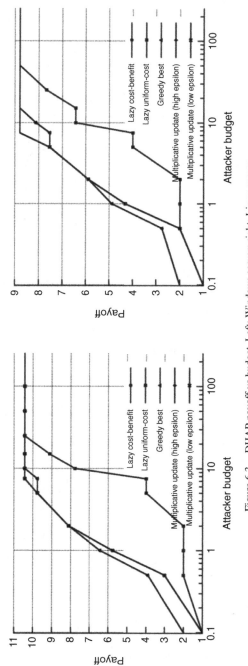

Figure 6.3. DHAP payoff vs budget. Left: Windows server; right: Linux server.

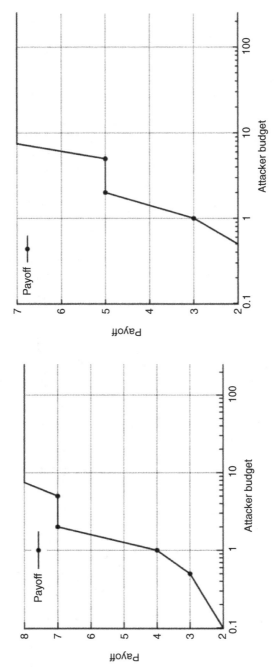

Figure 6.4. Defender best response, payoff vs k_{atk}. Left: Windows server; right: Linux server.

the payoff is generally lower, meaning that the defender can lower the expected payoff by enacting a best-response strategy to an attack strategy produced by DHAP—which in our framework translates to fewer exploited vulnerabilities.

6.5.5 Double-Oracle Results

Figure 6.5 depicts the results for the double-oracle algorithm presented in Algorithm 5. To instantiate the algorithm, a randomly generated defense strategy and attack strategy that satisfied the application constraints and the attack budget constraint, respectively, were used. The greedy DHAP algorithm (Algorithm 1) and the greedy weighted set cover algorithm (Algorithm 3) were used as the oracles for the attacker and defender, respectively. For the dataset discussed, the runtime of the double-oracle algorithm never exceeded one minute, though we expect this to change as the size of the dataset scales up. In Figure 6.5, we again see the intuitive trend that an increase in attacker budget results in an increase in payoff (expected payoff in this case) that was present in the deterministic problem results.

6.5.6 Exploit Payoff Analysis

Instead of altering the software that appears on the host system in an attempt to avoid exploits, such as in the best-response approach, in exploit payoff analysis, the defender will identify which specific exploits are increasing the payoff the most, with a hope that the defender can reverse-engineer the exploit, or patch the vulnerability himself. To identify which exploits should be reverse-engineered, the defender first runs DHAP against his host system to identify what payoff an attacker could expect to produce. Then, for each exploit ex, the defender runs DHAP against the host with the set of exploits $Ex\backslash\{ex\}$. The exploit ex that, when removed from the universe of exploits Ex, produces the largest drop in payoff for the attacker is the exploit that the defender should attempt to reverse-engineer. More formally, let A be the attack strategy produced by DHAP when using Ex as the universe of exploits and let A_{ex} be the attack strategy that is produced when DHAP is run against the host when using $Ex\backslash\{ex\}$ as the universe of exploits. The defender will attempt to reverse-engineer the exploit $ex = \text{argmax}_{ex \in Ex} p(A, D) - p(A_{ex}, D)$, where D is the defense strategy representing the host. To account for exploits that, though they greatly reduce payoff when removed from Ex, may be too expensive for the defender to purchase, we also consider a cost-benefit analysis, where the decrease in payoff is normalized by the cost of the exploit

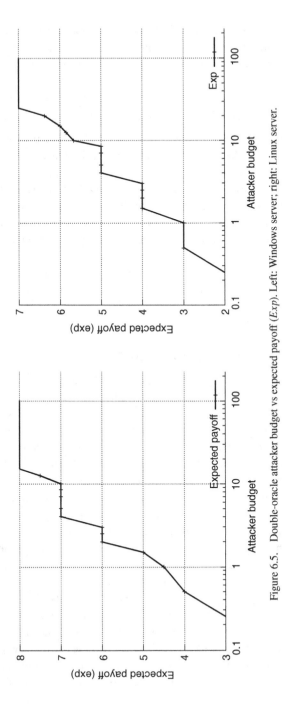

Figure 6.5. Double-oracle attacker budget vs expected payoff (*Exp*). Left: Windows server; right: Linux server.

Table 6.6. *Defender exploit analysis for $k_{atk} = 5$*

Exploit	Max. payoff reduction	Max. cost-benefit	Exploit cost (BTC)
SMTP Mail Cracker	1	4.757	0.2102
SUPEE-5433	1	1.190	0.8404
Hack ICQ	1	79.089	0.01264
Plasma	0.6677	1.582	0.2563
Wordpress Exploiter	0.6677	2.6467	0.2102
CVE-2014-0160	0.6677	3.178	0.2101

(i.e. $ex = \text{argmax}_{ex \in Ex} \frac{p(A,D) - p(A_{ex},D)}{c_{ex}}$). The top exploits to reverse-engineer to defend a Windows server host when considering an attacker budget of $k_{atk} = 5$, are shown in Table 6.6 with columns for both maximum payoff reduction and maximum cost-benefit analysis.

6.6 Conclusion

By extending the exploit function in the framework, we plan to support blended threats, where the number of vulnerabilities affected by a cyber-attack is a superset of the union of the vulnerabilities affected by each individual exploit (i.e. $ExF(A) \supseteq \bigcup_{a \in A} ExF(\{a\})$). Additionally, in future work, we plan to more closely integrate this framework with the darknet data-collection pipeline that we have, with an end goal of providing real-time game-theoretic policy recommendations to system administrators. One of the major hurdles in real-time integration is automating the mapping of darknet exploits to vulnerabilities (i.e. creating the exploit function).

This chapter presented a game theoretic framework capable of making system-specific policy recommendations derived from real-world darknet exploit data. This framework is another example of how we can use the darknet data from the hacker communities discussed in Chapters 3–5 to provide actionable cyber threat intelligence. In the next chapter we will discuss another application that leverages exploit information and detail a model that can be used in the defense of critical infrastructure.

7

Application: Protecting Industrial
Control Systems

7.1 Introduction

In the last chapter, we explored how to determine a cyber-attacker's optimal strategy for attacking a computer system based on malware and exploits available on the darkweb. In this chapter, we look at the case where the attacker is focused on industrial control systems (ICS): IT infrastructure that controls physical systems (electricity, water, industrial machinery, etc.). A critical feature of these complex ICS systems is the interdependencies among various components.

However, despite the prevalence of markets for malware and exploits, and their potential threat to ICS, existing paradigms, including the framework presented in the previous chapter, do not account for the complex nature of ICS systems consisting of multiple interconnected components. In particular, it would prove useful to simulate a cyber-attack on a model of an existing system, to assess its degree of vulnerability. Such a model would also prove useful for automated cybersecurity systems that can learn defense and contingency strategies based on the model's simulations. This chapter takes the first steps toward addressing this need. In particular, we introduce a framework that allows for modeling of ICS systems with highly interconnected components (Section 7.3) and study this model through the lens of lattice theory [57]. We then turn our attention to the problem of determining the optimal/most dangerous strategy for a cyber-adversary with respect to this model and find it to be an NP-Complete problem (Section 7.4). Next, we present a suite of algorithms for this problem based on A* search and introduce provably correct algorithms (Section 7.5). Our intuition is that these algorithms will obtain satisfactory performance in practice due to heuristic functions (for which we show admissibility). We demonstrate the performance of these algorithms by implementing them and performing a suite of experiments using both simulated and actual vulnerability data (Section 7.6). This chapter also includes some background on ICS (Section 7.2) and a brief overview of related work (Section 7.7).

7.2 Background

Contemporary cyber threat actors rely on a variety of malware and exploits purchased through various channels such as the darkweb [99] in order to carry out their attacks. The trend toward automation of industrial control systems (ICS) and toward "smart" utilities [50] has made understanding such adversarial-behavior directed against ICS a priority. For instance, code from the infamous Stuxnet [97] attack against Iranian nuclear facilities is available for public download.[1] The Stuxnet case is also informative as it illustrates the complex nature of industrial control systems that consist of interconnected components. For example, when Stuxnet infected Siemens S7-300 PLCs by exploiting various zero-day exploits on the Windows operating-system [53], it gained the ability to send commands to modify the rotational-frequency of motors that operated nuclear-centrifuges [53], and also gained the ability to hide its behavior from operators [33].

Industrial sectors and critical infrastructure use different kinds of automated systems, which are collectively known as *Industrial Control Systems* (ICS). The term describes different kinds of control systems, like supervisory-control and data-acquisition systems (SCADA), distributed control-systems (DCS), and other control-system configurations, such as skid-mounted PLCs [106]. Prior to the ubiquity of the Internet and networked-systems in general, ICS were insular systems using extremely specialized hardware and software that communicated using proprietary protocols. These systems were also physically secured and system components were not connected to computer networks. Over the last two decades, however, these systems have evolved; IT capabilities have been gradually added to existing systems to make them "smarter." Digital controls and software solutions have also replaced physical control-mechanisms.

This situation has changed even more dramatically due to the growth of the Internet, which has spurred an increase in the availability of low-cost physical-devices with embedded networking-capabilities. This has made it possible to create networks of these devices (which may even be geographically disparate) and integrate them into existing corporate-networks, providing a central interface for administration, control, monitoring, and data-collection. However in doing so, ICS have now come to resemble traditional IT systems [106] and, hence, are susceptible to the same vulnerabilities that affect those systems.

---

[1] https://archive.org/details/Stuxnet

Examples of such vulnerabilities include: susceptibility to DoS (Denial of Service) attacks, risk of infection by viruses and malware, and susceptibility to intrusion from unauthorized parties.

While traditional security-measures can help, a greater degree of vigilance is necessary in the case of ICS, since malicious actions can have physical consequences leading to loss of human life or damage to critical infrastructure. The nature of these physical consequences also makes these systems attractive targets for terrorists or hostile states; in contrast to isolated attacks from malicious individuals, dedicated attacks from hostile organizations pose a formidable threat since the attackers usually have access to better resources, leading to more-sophisticated forms of attacks. A well-known example is the Stuxnet worm; the high degree of sophistication displayed in the attack and the extremely specific set of strategic goals show that it could only have been developed through a large investment of time and money, and through the involvement of experts with varying specializations [53]. Stuxnet also shows how ICS share the same vulnerabilities as traditional IT systems, since it employed zero-day exploits to attack Windows systems, and also used internal networks as an infection vector.

A more-recent and immediately relevant example from December 2015 is the successful attack against Ukrainian ICS that control the country's electrical system [4]. The attack left at least 80,000 Ukrainians without electricity. The attack itself was quite sophisticated and used a piece of malware called BlackEnergy which took advantage of several vulnerabilities in the Ukrainian electrical-system's ICS. The attack is also unique in the sense that it seems to be the first example of a deliberate cyber-attack against the critical infrastructure of a nation, which also affected a large number of its citizens [4]. Similar malware has also been observed to be used against a Ukrainian miningcompany and Train/Railway operator [117]. In contrast, Stuxnet only attacked military targets and had minimum impact on civilian infrastructure. ICS networks can feature complicated-topologies that include various types of components; some of these components are not directly involved in the industrial process, but are instead part of network infrastructure (like routers) or emergency backup-power systems. Hence, to better understand how a cyber adversary will leverage malware and exploits available to him or her through illicit marketplaces, we will now present a model that can describe these kinds of attacker behaviors.

7.3 Model

ICS components are networked [106], and any publicly accessible component, or a component reachable through a publicly accessible component, is potentially vulnerable to attack. If the attacker was to compromise one of these devices, he or she could take control of that device and gain access to its functionality, or even disable the device completely by launching, for example, a denial-of-service attack against it. Even if the system employs privilege-checks or authentication mechanisms, it is possible for attackers to escalate their privileges through certain kinds of attacks, giving them access to privileged commands. In this section, we define a formal mathematical model to capture this behavior.

We first define a set V, which is the set of all vulnerabilities, and a set C, which is the set of capabilities supported by a component on the ICS network. The set 2^C is the powerset of C.

Example 7.3.1 *The identities of vulnerabilities have been standardized and they are collectively known as* Common Vulnerabilities and Exposures *(CVE) [69]; the vulnerabilities themselves are uniquely identified by a CVE number, and each entry contains detailed information, which includes the manner in which the vulnerability can be exploited (i.e., what commands to send), and the capabilities gained by an attacker from doing so (e.g., "remote code-execution" or "denial of service"). A set of CVE's (identified by their CVE number) is therefore a good example of the set V. Elements in set C are abstractions of available functionality on a system. As such, they do not necessarily represent an actual command recognized by the machine; an element could also represent a series of commands, a capability obtained by exploiting a vulnerability, a command combined with a capability (such as a remote code-execution exploit with a payload), or some sort of high-level interaction like an HTTP request. If we consider a Linux server with an unpatched Shellshock [112] vulnerability, running version 2.6 of the Linux kernel (susceptible to a privilege-escalation exploit [28]), the set V for this machine can be defined as* $\{2014 - 6271, 2009 - 1185\}$*, where the elements in the set denote the CVE numbers of associated vulnerabilities, and the set C defined as* {crafted_get, exec_uname, esc_priv, priv_reboot}.

Right away, we notice the following property:

Observation 7.3.1 $\langle \subseteq, 2^C \rangle$ *is a partial ordering and* 2^C *specifies a complete lattice.*

This is straightforward as $\subseteq$ is clearly reflexive, transitive, and antisymmetric. Further, the set 2^C has a clear top element (set C) and a bottom element (the empty set). As C is simply a set of elements, the powerset as under the ordering relationship specified by $\subseteq$ is the classic example of a complete lattice.

To exploit a system, an attacker sends a command or tries to leverage a capability that is associated with some vulnerability on the system. However, attackers usually have incomplete information about system vulnerabilities. By profiling a system through various methods, they can identify some set of vulnerabilities that exist, but this set does not necessarily contain *all* vulnerabilities on that system. That said, it is still possible for attackers to use additional commands or capabilities to expose vulnerabilities outside the set of initial, known vulnerabilities. We model this through the following function:

Definition 7.3.1 *We define $expose : 2^C \rightarrow 2^V$ as a function that satisfies the following axioms:*

1 If $C_1 \subseteq C_2$ then $expose(C_1) \subseteq expose(C_2)$
2 $expose(\varnothing) \not\equiv \varnothing$

The intuition behind the first axiom is that access to additional capabilities can allow the attacker to expose additional vulnerabilities; it can never result in the attacker *concealing* a previously-exposed vulnerability, and at worst the attacker ends up with the same set of exposed vulnerabilities as before.

Example 7.3.2 *Consider the machine described in Example 7.3.1. Let us assume that the attacker is trying see if a Shellshock vulnerability can be exposed by sending a crafted HTTP GET request that contains arbitrary code. Here, we have $C' = \{\texttt{crafted\_get}\}$ and $expose(C') = \{2014 - 6271\}$. Let us now assume that the attacker tries to find the server's Linux-kernel version to see if a privilege-escalation vulnerability can be exposed and exploited. That is, we have $C' = \{\texttt{crafted\_get}, \texttt{exec\_uname}\}$. The* uname *command returns the version of the Linux kernel, letting the attacker know that the system is susceptible to a privilege-escalation vulnerability. Hence, $expose(C') = \{2014 - 6271, 2009 - 1185\}$. We can see here that the attacker cannot expose more vulnerabilities by sending more commands, since there are only only two vulnerabilities on the system. Therefore, even if we assume that the attacker escalates his privilege and then runs the privileged* reboot *command, he still exposes the same set of vulnerabilities. That is, if we have $C' = C = \{\texttt{crafted\_get}, \texttt{exec\_uname}, \texttt{esc\_priv}, \texttt{priv\_reboot}\}$, then $expose(C') = V$.*

The intuition behind the second axiom is that it is possible for attackers to have prior information about existing vulnerabilities on a system. Hence, it follows from our definition that $expose(C)$ is the complete set of vulnerabilities that exist on this system, and $expose(\varnothing)$ is the set of initial, known vulnerabilities.

Example 7.3.3 *Consider again, the machine described in Example 7.3.1. Instead of having to find the vulnerability, let us assume that the attacker has prior knowledge that the system is susceptible to Shellshock. In this case $C' = \varnothing$ and $expose(C') = \{2014 - 6271\}$, meaning that even without access* *to any commands and capabilities on the system, the Shellshock vulnerability is still exposed to the attacker.*

The end goal of the attacker is to gain capabilities by using exploits against the system they are attacking. These capabilities include access to local commands on the system, as well as commands that can be used to exploit specific-vulnerabilities (e.g., sending malformed data to cause a denial-of-service attack). To model this behavior, we first define the set of exploits E as follows:

Definition 7.3.2 *Given a set C_1 of capabilities that the attacker has already gained so far, and a set C_2 of capabilities gained by exploiting vulnerability v, the set of exploits E is a set of tuples of the form $\langle C_1, C_2, v \rangle$.*

For some set of exploits $E' \subseteq E$ available to the attacker, we now define the operator $\mathbf{T}_{E'} : 2^C \rightarrow 2^C$ as follows:

Definition 7.3.3 *Given $E' \subseteq E$ and $C' \in 2^C$ we define the operator $\mathbf{T}_{E'} : 2^C \rightarrow 2^C$ as:*

$$\mathbf{T}_{E'}(C') = C' \cup \bigcup \{C_2 \mid \langle C_1, C_2, v \rangle \in E' \wedge$$

$$C_1 \subseteq C' \wedge$$

$$v \in expose(C')\}.$$

Example 7.3.4 *Assume that the attacker has a set of exploits E' that consists of the following tuples:*

- *$\langle \varnothing, \{\texttt{crafted\_get}\}, 2014 - 6271 \rangle$*
- *$\langle \varnothing, \{\texttt{crafted\_tkey, dos}\}, 2015 - 5477 \rangle$*
- *$\langle \{\texttt{crafted\_get}\}, \{\texttt{exec\_uname}\}, 2014 - 6271 \rangle$*
- *$\langle \{\texttt{crafted\_get, exec\_uname}\}, \{\texttt{esc\_priv}\}, 2009 - 1185 \rangle$*
- *$\langle \{\texttt{crafted\_get, exec\_uname, esc\_priv}\}, \{\texttt{priv\_reboot}\}, 2009 - 1185 \rangle$*

Assuming that the attacker's initial set of capabilities $C' = \varnothing$, consider what happens when we apply $\mathbf{T}_{E'}$ against the machine described in Example 7.3.1 with an expose function as described in Example 7.3.2. Right away we can see that the only exploit that satisfies the conditions in Definition 7.3.3 is $\langle \varnothing, \{\texttt{crafted\_get}\}, 2014 - 6271 \rangle$. Hence we have:

$$\mathbf{T}_{E'}(C') = \mathbf{T}_{E'}(\varnothing)$$

$$= \varnothing \cup \bigcup \{\{\texttt{crafted\_get}\}\}$$

$$= \{\texttt{crafted\_get}\}.$$

This means that the attacker has now gained the ability to send crafted HTTP GET requests that exploit the Shellshock vulnerability.

An attacker can progressively gain more capabilities as he uses his set of exploits against the system. We can model this through repeated applications of $\mathbf{T}_{E'}$, defined as follows:

Definition 7.3.4 *Given some $i \in \mathbb{Z}$ where $i > 0$, we define i applications of $\mathbf{T}_{E'}$ on $C' \subseteq C$ as:*

$$\mathbf{T}_{E'} \uparrow_i (C') = \mathbf{T}_{E'}(\mathbf{T}_{E'} \uparrow_{i-1} (C'))$$

$$where \ \mathbf{T}_{E'} \uparrow_0 (C') = \mathbf{T}_{E'}(C').$$

Example 7.3.5 *Assuming the same situation described in Example 7.3.4, consider what happens after four applications of $\mathbf{T}_{E'}$. For the initial application of $\mathbf{T}_{E'}$ we have:*

$$\mathbf{T}_{E'} \uparrow_0 (C') = \mathbf{T}_{E'}(C') \qquad \qquad (Definition \ 7.3.4)$$

$$= \{\texttt{crafted\_get}\}. \qquad \qquad (Example \ 7.3.4)$$

The second time we apply $\mathbf{T}_{E'}$, exploit $\langle\{\texttt{crafted\_get}\}, \{\texttt{exec\_uname}\}, 2014 - 6271\rangle$ satisfies the conditions in Definition 7.3.3, hence:

$$\mathbf{T}_{E'} \uparrow_1 (C') = \mathbf{T}_{E'}(\mathbf{T}_{E'} \uparrow_0 (C'))$$

$$= \mathbf{T}_{E'}(\{\texttt{crafted\_get}\})$$

$$= \{\texttt{crafted\_get}\} \cup \bigcup\{\{\texttt{exec\_uname}\}\}$$

$$= \{\texttt{crafted\_get}, \texttt{exec\_uname}\}.$$

Similarly in the third application, with exploit $\langle\{\texttt{crafted\_get}, \texttt{exec\_uname}\}, \{\texttt{esc\_priv}\}, 2009 - 1185\rangle$ satisfying conditions in Definition 7.3.3, we have:

$$\mathbf{T}_{E'} \uparrow_2 (C') = \mathbf{T}_{E'}(\mathbf{T}_{E'} \uparrow_1 (C'))$$

$$= \mathbf{T}_{E'}(\{\texttt{crafted\_get}, \texttt{exec\_uname}\})$$

$$= \{\texttt{crafted\_get}, \texttt{exec\_uname}\} \cup$$

$$\bigcup\{\{\texttt{esc\_priv}\}\}$$

$$= \{\texttt{crafted\_get}, \texttt{exec\_uname},$$

$$\texttt{esc\_priv}\}.$$

Finally, with exploit $\langle\{\texttt{crafted\_get}, \texttt{exec\_uname}, \texttt{esc\_priv}\}, \{\texttt{priv\_reboot}\}, 2009 - 1185\rangle$ satisfying conditions in Definition 7.3.3, *we have:*

$$\mathbf{T}_{E'} \uparrow_3 (C') = \mathbf{T}_{E'}(\mathbf{T}_{E'} \uparrow_2 (C'))$$

$$= \mathbf{T}_{E'}(\{\texttt{crafted\_get}, \texttt{exec\_uname},$$

$$\texttt{esc\_priv}\})$$

$$= \{\texttt{crafted\_get}, \texttt{exec\_uname},$$

$$\texttt{esc\_priv}\} \cup \bigcup\{\{\texttt{priv\_reboot}\}\}$$

$$= \{\texttt{crafted\_get}, \texttt{exec\_uname},$$

$$\texttt{esc\_priv}, \texttt{priv\_reboot}\}.$$

This demonstrates that after the fourth application of $\mathbf{T}_{E'}$, the attacker has gained access to all capabilities on the system. That is, $\mathbf{T}_{E'} \uparrow_3 (C') = C$.

Using the definition of the repeated application of $\mathbf{T}_{E'}$, we can define its fixed point as follows:

Definition 7.3.5 $\mathbf{T}_{E'}^*$, *the fixed point of $\mathbf{T}_{E'}$ is defined as:*

$$\mathbf{T}_{E'}^*(C') = \mathbf{T}_{E'} \uparrow_i (C') \text{ where:}$$

$$\mathbf{T}_{E'} \uparrow_i (C') = \mathbf{T}_{E'} \uparrow_{i+1} (C').$$

Example 7.3.6 *It is evident that the fixed point was reached in Example 7.3.5, since the attacker gained access to all capabilities on the system after the fourth application of $\mathbf{T}_{E'}$. Further applications provide no additional benefit as there are no more capabilities to be gained. Hence $\mathbf{T}_{E'}^*(C') = \mathbf{T}_{E'} \uparrow_3 (C')$.*

We will now prove that this fixed point exists.

Theorem 1 $\mathbf{T}_{E'}^*$ *has a least fixed point.*

Proof

Claim 1 ($C' \subseteq \mathbf{T}_{E'}(C')$.) *Let C' be the attacker's existing set of capabilities. From Definition 7.3.3, we can say that $\mathbf{T}_{E'}(C')$ is the union of C' and another set. Hence $\mathbf{T}_{E'}$ is order increasing.*

Claim 2 (If $C' \subseteq C''$ then $\mathbf{T}_{E'}(C') \subseteq \mathbf{T}_{E'}(C'')$.) *By way of contradiction, assume that we have C', C'' where $C' \subseteq C''$ and $\mathbf{T}_{E'}(C') \not\subseteq \mathbf{T}_{E'}(C'')$. Let $C'' = C' \cup X$*

where $X = C'' \setminus C'$, and for brevity:

$$X' = \bigcup \{C_2 \mid \langle C_1, C_2, v \rangle \in E' \wedge$$

$$C_1 \subseteq C' \wedge$$

$$v \in expose(C')\}$$

$$X'' = \bigcup \{C_2 \mid \langle C_1, C_2, v \rangle \in E' \wedge$$

$$C_1 \subseteq C'' \wedge$$

$$v \in expose(C'')\}.$$

Then:

$$\mathbf{T}_{E'}(C'') = C'' \cup X''.$$

Note that $C' \subseteq C''$, which means that $X' \subseteq X''$. Hence, we can do the following:

$$\mathbf{T}_{E'}(C'') = C' \cup X \cup X'' \cup X'.$$

After rearranging, we have:

$$\mathbf{T}_{E'}(C'') = C' \cup X' \cup X \cup X''.$$

Since the union operation only adds elements to a set, we can conclude that $\mathbf{T}_{E'}(C') \subseteq \mathbf{T}_{E'}(C'')$, which contradicts our assumption and therefore proves monotonicity.

Proof of theorem: By Observation 7.3.1, and claims 1 and 2, we can apply Knaster-Tarski [57] which means that $\mathbf{T}_{E'}$ has a least fixed point. □

An attacker uses a set of exploits to gain capabilities on the system, and must do so within a budget. But first, we need a way to calculate the cost associated with a set of exploits:

Definition 7.3.6 *Given a set of exploits E, we define a cost function cost : $E \to \mathbb{R}^+$ that associates a real-valued cost with each exploit.*

For simplicity, we will use a single cost-function throughout this chapter. However, all of the results can be extended for separate cost-functions for the attacker. Also, throughout this chapter, we will use a unit cost-function, where for each $e \in E$, $cost(e) = 1$. In ongoing work, we are currently looking at data-driven cost functions [90], and our theoretical results do not depend on the use of the unit cost-function. A logical next step is to incorporate the price information of exploits from darknet markets into this model. Having defined the *cost* function, we can now formally define the attacker's preferred strategy:

Definition 7.3.7 *Given the attacker's budget $c \in \mathbb{R}^+$, set of desired capabilities C', and initial set of capabilities C'', the* **preferred attack-strategy** *is the set of exploits E' satisfying the following conditions:*

- $\mathbf{T}_{E'}^*(C'') \supseteq C'$
- $\sum_{e \in E'} cost(e) \leq c.$

In the optimization variant of the preferred attack-strategy problem, the quantity $\sum_{e \in E'} cost(e)$ is minimized, and the associated strategy is called the **optimal strategy**.

7.4 Computational Complexity

In this section, we examine the computational complexity of solving the preferred attack-strategy problem. We will show that finding a preferred attack-strategy is NP-complete.

Theorem 2 *Finding a preferred attack-strategy is NP-complete*

Proof

Claim 1 (Finding a preferred attack-strategy is in-NP.) *Finding the preferred attack-strategy is clearly in NP. Given the attacker's set of desired capabilities C', initial set of capabilities C'', set of exploits E', and budget c, we can calculate $\mathbf{T}_{E'}^*(C'')$ and the total exploit-cost in polynomial time to verify that E' is the preferred attack-strategy.*

Claim 2 (Finding a preferred attack-strategy is NP-hard.) *We can show that finding the preferred attack-strategy is NP-hard by constructing an instance of the problem from an instance of the Set Cover problem. The Set Cover problem is stated as follows: given a set of sets $U = \{S_1, S_2, \ldots, S_n\}$ and a number k, find a $S' \subseteq U$ such that $|S'| \leq k$ and $\bigcup_{S_i \in S'} S_i = \bigcup_{S_i \in U} S_i$.*

Construction: *We will construct an instance of the preferred attack-strategy problem from an arbitrary instance of the Set Cover problem using the algorithm SETCOVER2PAS, which is defined as follows:*

- *Build the set of vulnerabilities $V = \{v_i \mid S_i \in U\}$.*
- *Build the global set of capabilities and the attacker's desired set of capabilities $C = C' = \bigcup_{S_i \in U} S_i$.*
- *Build the set of available exploits $E = \{\langle \varnothing, S_i, v_i \rangle \mid S_i \in U\}$.*
- *Set the attacker's initial set of capabilities $C'' = \varnothing$, and the attacker's budget $c = k$.*

- *We define the cost-function for any exploit $e \in E$ as $cost(e) = 1$.*
- *We define expose for any set of capabilities $X \subseteq C$ as $expose(X) = V$.*

Claim 2.1 SETCOVER2PAS *runs in polynomial time.*

The algorithm SETCOVER2PAS *clearly runs in polynomial time (specifically $O(|U|)$), since the construction of each of the sets described in the algorithm only requires us to iterate over elements in U.*

Claim 2.2 *If there is a solution to the Set Cover problem, then there exists a preferred attack-strategy.*

Suppose by way of contradiction, there is a set cover S' of U such that $|S'| \leq k$, which does not have a corresponding preferred-attack strategy. By our construction, S' corresponds to a set of exploits $E' = \{\langle \varnothing, S_i, v_i \rangle \mid S_i \in S'\}$. Since we set $c = k$, E' clearly contains at most c exploits, and therefore $\sum_{e \in E'} cost(e) \leq c$. We also know that $\mathbf{T}_{E'}(C'') = \mathbf{T}_{E'}(\varnothing) = \varnothing \cup \bigcup \{S_i \mid \langle \varnothing, S_i, v_i \rangle \in E'\}$, since every exploit satisfies the conditions in Definition 7.3.3. Hence one iteration of $\mathbf{T}_{E'}$ is the fixed point and:

$$\mathbf{T}_{E'}^*(\varnothing) = \mathbf{T}_{E'}(\varnothing)$$

$$= \varnothing \cup \bigcup \{S_i \mid \langle \varnothing, S_i, v_i \rangle \in E'\}$$

$$= \bigcup_{S_i \in S'} S_i.$$

Based on our construction, we also know that $C = C' = \bigcup_{S_i \in U} S_i$. Since S' is a cover of U, it follows that $\bigcup_{S_i \in S'} S_i = \bigcup_{S_i \in U} S_i$. But we have shown that $\mathbf{T}_{E'}^*(C'') = \bigcup_{S_i \in S'} S_i$, which means that $\mathbf{T}_{E'}^*(C'') = C = C'$. Therefore E', which corresponds to a solution S' of the Set Cover problem, is the preferred attack-strategy. *Hence, a contradiction.*

Claim 2.3 *If there is no solution to the Set Cover problem, then there does not exist a preferred attack-strategy.*

Suppose by way of contradiction, there is a preferred attack-strategy E' without a corresponding solution to the Set Cover problem. For the constructed problem, the fixed-point operator always converges after a single iteration, giving us $\mathbf{T}_{E'}^*(C'') = \bigcup \{S_i \mid \langle \varnothing, S_i, v_i \rangle \in E'\}$. From Definition 7.3.7, and given that the desired set of capabilities is defined as $C' = \bigcup_{S_i \in S'} S_i$ in the constructed problem, $\mathbf{T}_{E'}^*(C'') \supseteq C'$, which also implies that it is a cover. Likewise, we also know that $|E'| \leq k$. Therefore $\mathbf{T}_{E'}^*(C'')$ satisfies the criteria to be a cover, which implies that a solution S' to the Set Cover problem must exist. Hence, a contradiction.

Proof of theorem: Follows directly from claims 1 and 2.   □

7.5 Algorithms

In this section, we examine several algorithms to solve the preferred attack-strategy problem. We first examine a baseline approach PAS-DFS (see Algorithm 6) that performs a depth-first search across the strategy-space. It is immediately evident that this approach has shortcomings; we are not guaranteed to find an optimal solution. Additionally, this approach takes exponential-time complexity. Given that branching-factor of the search-tree is $|E|$, and since the maximum number of exploits that can be used is also $|E|$, time complexity is $O(|E|^{|E|})$, and space complexity is $O(|E|^2)$. Regardless of these shortcomings, PAS-BFS can be used as an anytime algorithm and is guaranteed to return a solution, though not necessarily optimal. However, as the algorithm continues to search, it can return better solutions. We provide two improvements over standard DFS to enable more efficient searches for attacker strategies:

1 We correctly prune the available exploits at each step.
2 We employ the use of an admissible heuristic-function by adopting A* search.

All of these improvements allow us to maintain the correctness of the approach.

7.5.1 Pruning Exploits

The exponential branching-factor in PAS-DFS is due to the fact that it needlessly expands nonviable subtrees that it could otherwise ignore. To address this problem, we can use the algorithm PAS-DFS-PRUNED (see Algorithm 7), which prunes nonviable subtrees by discarding exploits that cannot be part of a solution. When expanding a node, PAS-DFS-PRUNED determines the viability of a subtree corresponding to an available exploit by ensuring that the following conditions hold:

1 The cost of the exploit does not cause the attacker to exceed their budget.
2 The attacker has the required set of capabilities to apply the exploit.
3 The exploit offers capabilities that the attacker does not already have.

Only if these three conditions hold will PAS-DFS-PRUNED include the exploit; otherwise it will prune the corresponding subtree. The correctness of this

---

Algorithm 6 DFS algorithm to find preferred attacker-strategy

---

 1: **procedure** PAS-DFS(E, C'', C', c):
 2:     **function** PATH($node$):
 3:         *path* **as** SET
 4:         **while** $node$.PARENT $\neq \varnothing$ **do**:
 5:             ADD(*path*, $node$.EXPLOIT)
 6:             $node \leftarrow node$.PARENT
 7:         **return** *path*
 8:     **function** SOLUTION($node$):
 9:         **return** PATH($node$)
10:     **function** ROOT:
11:         *root* **as** NODE
12:         *root*.PARENT $\leftarrow \varnothing$
13:         *root*.EXPLOIT $\leftarrow \varnothing$
14:         *root*.PATHCOST $\leftarrow 0$
15:         **return** *root*
16:     **function** MAKENODE($parent$, e):
17:         *node* **as** NODE
18:         $node$.PARENT $\leftarrow parent$
19:         $node$.EXPLOIT $\leftarrow e$
20:         $node$.PATHCOST $\leftarrow parent$.PATHCOST $+ cost(e)$
21:         **return** *node*
22:     *nodes* **as** LIFO-QUEUE
23:     ENQUEUE(*nodes*, ROOT)
24:     **loop do**:
25:         **if** EMPTY(*nodes*) **then**:
26:             **return** *failure*
27:         $node \leftarrow$ DEQUEUE(*nodes*)
28:         $E' \leftarrow$ SOLUTION($node$)
29:         **if** $node$.PATHCOST $\leq c$ **and** $\mathbf{T}^*_{E'}(C'') \supseteq C'$ **then**:
30:             **return** E'
31:         **for each** e **in** $E \setminus$ PATH($node$):
32:             ENQUEUE(*nodes*, MAKENODE($node$, e))

---

pruning technique follows directly from our original model—hence we state the following proposition:

Proposition 7.5.1 PAS-DFS-PRUNED *correctly prunes nonviable subtrees and finds a correct solution if one exists.*

Algorithm 7 DFS with pruning (common functions omitted)

1:   **procedure** PAS-DFS-PRUNED(E, C'', C', c):
2:      **function** PRUNE(*parent*, *e*):
3:         **if** *parent*.PATHCOST $+ cost(e) > c$ **then**:
4:            **return** *true*
5:         **else if** $e.C_1 \not\subseteq \mathbf{T}^*_{E'}(C'')$ **then**:
6:            **return** *true*
7:         **else if** $e.C_2 \subseteq \mathbf{T}^*_{E'}(C'')$ **then**:
8:            **return** *true*
9:         **return** *false*
10:      **function** EXPAND(*node*):
11:         *children* **as** SET
12:         **for each** *e* **in** $E \setminus$ PATH(*node*):
13:            **if not** PRUNE(*node*, *e*) **then**:
14:               ADD(*children*, MAKENODE(*node*, *e*))
15:         **return** *children*
16:      *nodes* **as** LIFO-QUEUE
17:      ENQUEUE(*nodes*, ROOT)
18:      **loop do**:
19:         **if** EMPTY(*nodes*) **then**:
20:            **return** *failure*
21:         *node* $\leftarrow$ DEQUEUE(*nodes*)
22:         $E' \leftarrow$ SOLUTION(*node*)
23:         **if** $\mathbf{T}^*_{E'}(C'') \supseteq C'$ **then**:
24:            **return** E'
25:         **for each** *child* **in** EXPAND(*node*):
26:            ENQUEUE(*nodes*, *child*)

Proof We prove the statement of the theorem by first stating the precondition, loop invariant, and postcondition, and showing that these hold during all iterations.

Precondition: *nodes* is a LIFO queue of nodes that contains a root node of a search-tree that may or may not contain correct solutions.

Loop invariant: Aside from the root node, all nodes in *nodes* are either roots of viable subtrees or goal-state nodes.

Postcondition: If search-tree does not contain any correct solutions, the algorithm reports a failure; otherwise the algorithm reports the corresponding solution.

We will now show that these conditions hold during all iterations:

Initialization: At the first iteration, *nodes* initially contains only the root node. Hence, the invariant holds.

Maintenance: At iteration n, we assume that *nodes* contains roots of viable subtrees or goal-state nodes. Note that at iteration $n + 1$, we can pick a node *node* out of *nodes* if it is not empty. While the algorithm terminates if *node* is a goal-state node or if *nodes* was empty, the invariant still holds because *nodes* is not modified in either case. If *node* is not a goal-state node, we make a call to EXPAND where we create and return corresponding-nodes for only those exploits where the call to PRUNE returned *false*. Since we know that PRUNE disregards those exploits that cannot be part of a solution, each corresponding-node that we add to *nodes* must either represent a viable subtree or a goal-state node. Hence the invariant holds at iteration $n + 1$ as well.

Termination: Note that the algorithm terminates if *nodes* is empty or if the head node satisfies the goal test. In the former case, it implies that the search tree did not contain any correct solutions, because otherwise *nodes* would have had a goal-state node at the head during some iteration. In the latter case it implies that the search-tree has at least one correct-solution, because the head-node was a goal-state node; in either case both the loop invariant and the postcondition hold.

Since the precondition, loop invariant, and postcondition hold during all iterations, the algorithm PAS-DFS-PRUNED not only prunes nonviable subtrees correctly, but will return a correct solution if one exists.   □

7.5.2 A* and Admissible Heuristics

We can see that PAS-DFS-PRUNED helps us address time-complexity by pruning nonviable subtrees. However, it still does not guarantee us an optimal solution. One way to address this issue is by using an A* search across the strategy space. With an admissible heuristic-function, the tree-search variant of A* is both complete and optimal. We know that the attacker wants to find the most-inexpensive set of exploits that provide all of the desired capabilities. Therefore, a sensible heuristic would be to select an applicable exploit that is both inexpensive, and gives us the desired set of capabilities we want. A* evaluates nodes by combining $g(e)$, the cost to reach the node, and $h(e)$, the lower bound of the cost to get from the node to the goal. Since we cannot know the estimated cost to the goal without knowing what the attacker already has, we have to define a few other things before formally defining $h(e)$, namely, the remaining set of commands and exploits:

Definition 7.5.1 *Given the attacker's current set of exploits E', initial set of capabilities C'', desired set of capabilities C', and the applicable-exploit under consideration $\langle C_1, C_2, v \rangle$, we define the remaining set of desired capabilities C_{rem} as:*

$$C_{rem} = C' \setminus \mathbf{T}^*_{E'}(C'') \setminus C_2.$$

Definition 7.5.2 *Given the complete set of exploits E, the attacker's current set of exploits E', initial set of capabilities C'', and the applicable-exploit under consideration e, we define the remaining set of exploits E_{rem} as:*

$$E_{rem} = \{\langle C_1, C_2, v \rangle \mid \langle C_1, C_2, v \rangle \in E \setminus E' \setminus \{e\} \wedge$$

$$C_1 \subseteq \mathbf{T}^*_{E'}(C'') \wedge C_2 \cap C_{rem} \neq \varnothing\}.$$

We will now define two heuristics that estimate the cost to the goal, given a node representing an exploit:

Definition 7.5.3 *Given the node e that represents an applicable-exploit under consideration, the remaining set of capabilities C_{rem}, and the remaining set of exploits E_{rem}, the estimated cost to the goal $h_1 : E \rightarrow \mathbb{R}^+$ is defined as:*

$$h_1(e) = \min_{e' \in E_{rem}} \frac{cost(e')}{|C_2 \cap C_{rem}|} \times |C_{rem}|$$

where $e' = \langle C_1, C_2, v \rangle$.

We estimate the cost to the goal from e by calculating the minimum ratio between the cost of an exploit and the number of remaining capabilities it provides, for each remaining exploit, and then multiplying that value by the total number of remaining capabilities.

Definition 7.5.4 *Given the node e that represents an applicable-exploit under consideration, the remaining set of commands C_{rem}, and the remaining set of exploits E_{rem}, the estimated cost to the goal $h_2 : E \rightarrow \mathbb{R}^+$ is defined as:*

$$h_2(e) = \sum_{c \in C_{rem}} \min_{\{e' \in E_{rem} \mid c \in C_2\}} \frac{cost(e')}{|C_2 \cap C_{rem}|}$$

where $e' = \langle C_1, C_2, v \rangle$.

Here, we estimate the cost to the goal from e by finding, for each remaining capability, and for each remaining exploit that contains that capability, the minimum ratio between the cost of the exploit and the number of remaining capabilities it provides, and then summing those values.

Theorem 3 $h_1(e)$ *is admissible*

Proof We prove the statement of the theorem by showing that $h_1(e)$ is a lower bound of the true cost from node e to the goal.

Consider an optimal path to the goal from node e with true cost $h^*(e)$. Now for each remaining capability, build a set of exploits E' by picking the least-expensive exploit; for each $i \in C_{rem}$, let $e_i = \langle C_i, C_{i'}, v \rangle$ be the associated exploit. Note that $\sum_{e \in E'} cost(e) \leq h^*(e)$. Furthermore, note that $h_1(e)$ uses the cheapest exploit out of all remaining exploits and therefore $h_1(e) \leq \sum_{e \in E'} cost(e)$. Hence $h_1(e) \leq h^*(e)$, which means that it never overestimates the true cost to the goal, and is admissible.   □

Theorem 4 $h_2(e)$ *is admissible.*

Proof We prove the statement of the theorem by showing that $h_2(e)$ is a lower bound of the true cost from node e to the goal.

Consider an optimal path to the goal from node e with true cost $h^*(e)$. Now for each remaining capability, build a set of exploits E' by picking the least-expensive exploit; for each $i \in C_{rem}$, let $e_i = \langle C_i, C_{i'}, v \rangle$ be the associated exploit. Note that $\sum_{e \in E'} cost(e) \leq h^*(e)$. Further note that $\sum_{i \in C_{rem}} \frac{cost(e_i)}{|C_{rem} \cap C_{i'}|}$ must also be less than $h^*(e)$, and is also greater than $h_2(e)$. Hence $h_2(e) \leq h^*(e)$, which means that it never overestimates the true cost to the goal, and is admissible.   □

PAS-A* (see Algorithm 8) is an implementation of A* that supports either heuristic (implemented as MINCOST and RESTRICTEDMINCOST) based on the one supplied to the algorithm. Given that we have proved both heuristics to be admissible, PAS-A* is guaranteed to produce an optimal solution.

7.6 Experimental Results

In this section, we examine the results of experiments conducted to evaluate the performance of the algorithms described in the previous section. We performed two experiments: one with simulated data to evaluate the performance of the algorithms at various solution-depths, and the other to evaluate the general performance against actual CVE data gathered from NIST NVD. For the first experiment, we randomly generated a sets of exploits and desired-capabilities out of actual CVE data, that would guarantee a solution at a particular depth, whereas the second experiment used a subset of CVE data that we gathered from NIST NVD. Since our focus is on vulnerabilities identified through CVE's, we use the unit cost-function as the NIST NVD does not include exploit price-data.

Algorithm 8 Configurable A* that supports either heuristic

1: **procedure** PAS-A*(E, C'', C', c, h):
2:     **function** REMAININGCAPABILITIES($node$):
3:         $E' \leftarrow$ PATH($node$)
4:         **return** $C' \setminus \mathbf{T}_{E'}^*(C'')$
5:     **function** REMAININGEXPLOITS($node$):
6:         E_{rem} **as** SET
7:         **for each** e **in** $E \setminus$ PATH($node$):
8:             **if not** PRUNE($node, e$) **then**:
9:                 ADD(E_{rem}, e)
10:         **return** E_{rem}
11:     **function** ESTIMATEDCOST($node$):
12:         $C_{rem} \leftarrow$ REMAININGCAPABILITIES($node$)
13:         $E_{rem} \leftarrow$ REMAININGEXPLOITS($node$)
14:         **return** $node.$PATHCOST $+ h(C_{rem}, E_{rem})$
15:     *nodes* **as** PRIORITY-QUEUE   **ordered by** ESTIMATEDCOST
16:     ENQUEUE($nodes$, ROOT)
17:     **loop do**:
18:         **if** EMPTY($nodes$) **then**:
19:             **return** *failure*
20:         $node \leftarrow$ DEQUEUE($nodes$)
21:         $E' \leftarrow$ SOLUTION($node$)
22:         **if** $\mathbf{T}_{E'}^*(C'') \supseteq C'$ **then**:
23:             **return** E'
24:         **for each** *child* **in** EXPAND($node$):
25:             **if not** EXISTS($nodes$, *child*) **then**:
26:                 ENQUEUE($nodes$, *child*)
27:             **else**:
28:                 *existing* $\leftarrow$ FIND($nodes$, *child*)
29:                 $f_{existing} \leftarrow$ ESTIMATEDCOST($existing$)
30:                 $f_{child} \leftarrow$ ESTIMATEDCOST(*child*)
31:                 **if** $f_{child} < f_{existing}$ **then**:
32:                     REPLACE($nodes$, *existing*, *child*)
33: **function** MINCOST(C_{rem}, E_{rem}):
34:     h **as** REAL
35:     $h \leftarrow \infty$
36:     **for each** e **in** E_{rem}:
37:         $h_e \leftarrow (cost(e) \div |e.C_2 \cap C_{rem}|) \times |C_{rem}|$
38:         **if** $h_e < h$ **then**:
39:             $h \leftarrow h_e$
40:     **return** h

1: **function** RESTRICTEDMINCOST(C_{rem}, E_{rem}):
2:    h **as** REAL
3:    $h \leftarrow \infty$
4:    **for each** c **in** C_{rem}:
5:       **for each** e **in** E_{rem}:
6:          **if** $c \in e.C_2$ **then**:
7:             $h_e \leftarrow cost(e) \div |e.C_2 \cap C_{rem}|$
8:             **if** $h_e < h$ **then**:
9:                $h \leftarrow h_e$
10:   **return** h

In our first experiment, we ran algorithms PAS-DFS, PAS-DFS-PRUNED, and PAS-A* with both heuristics, against problems with solution depths 1 through 10; the results can seen in Table 7.1. Since we use the unit cost-function, the solution-depth is equal to to the attacker's budget. The set of exploits, 1139 in total, remained the same in each of the problem instances, with the only difference being the attacker's set of desired capabilities. Maximum execution-time for all algorithms were capped at one hour. We can see that performance gradually improves across PAS-DFS, PAS-DFS-PRUNED, PAS-A* with h_1, and PAS-A* with h_2, with the best overall-performance being seen in PAS-A* with h_2. As expected, the effective branching-factor also improves, demonstrating that the heuristics successfully prune the search space. Comparing the performance of the heuristic functions used in PAS-A*, we can see that h_2 significantly outperforms h_1, with a lower effective branching-factor and runtime. In cases with solution depths greater than 6, PAS-A* with h_1 failed to complete within an hour, whereas the runtime with h_2 was not affected significantly. This result suggests that h_2 makes an excellent heuristic to direct the search.

In our second experiment, we ran all algorithms against a subset of exploits, 458 in total, generated out of CVE data gathered from NIST NVD, with the attacker budget set at 4 (results in Table 7.2). The desired capabilities for the attacker were set to include an authentication-bypass capability, an arbitrary command-execution capability, a privilege-escalation capability, and one or more privileged-commands. Our results were as expected, except in the case of PAS-DFS-PRUNED, which seems to outperform PAS-A* when comparing runtimes. However, this is an artifact of the data since in contrast to our randomly-generated exploits, a large number of exploits gathered from NIST NVD data had no required capabilities. Hence if PAS-DFS-PRUNED happens to choose a subtree from the root that offers a quick path to the solution, it can outperform

Table 7.1. *Comparison of runtime and effective branching-factor for solution depths 1 through 10 for all algorithms*

Budget	A* using h_2		A* using h_1		DFS-Pruned		DFS	
	Runtime	b*	Runtime	b*	Runtime	b*	Runtime	b*
1	44ms	7.416	16ms	7.416	35ms	7.416	32ms	33.749
2	43ms	6.028	128ms	6.028	226ns	12.203	346ms	50.190
3	175ms	4.649	228ms	5.987	4.6s	15.259	7m17s	133.456
4	365ms	4.179	232ms	4.179	30m	28.143	–	–
5	650ms	3.69	38.425s	7.209	–	–	–	–
6	707ms	3.09	1m20s	5.978	–	–	–	–
7	2.518s	3.122	–	–	–	–	–	–
8	6.819s	3.016	–	–	–	–	–	–
9	6.206s	2.684	–	–	–	–	–	–
10	28.894s	2.789	–	–	–	–	–	–

Table 7.2.   *Comparison of runtime and effective branching-factor on a subset of NIST NVD data for all algorithms*

Algorithm	Runtime	b*
PAS-A* with h_2	13.634s	5.018
PAS-A* with h_1	8m30s	10.220
DFS-PRUNED	4.468s	5.501
DFS	2m23s	13.522

PAS-A*. In general, however, it will not perform as well, as can be seen from the effective branching-factor for both algorithms; even with a lower runtime, PAS-DFS-PRUNED has an effective branching-factor of around 5.5, compared to 5 for PAS-A*. Something similar happens in the case of PAS-DFS when compared to PAS-A* with h_1. In this case, PAS-DFS has a significantly lower runtime, but its branching factor is around 13.5, compared to 10 for PAS-A* with h_1.

7.7 Related Work

In recent years, many contributions have been made in the field of cyber-security, especially from a game-theoretic perspective, using attacker-defender models to inform defender-actions. With regard to ICS, work has been done on modeling adversary-initiated cascading-failures in power-grid [98] and critical-infrastructure systems in general [38], to identify defender strategies to mitigate these failures. In the same area, work has been done with the aim of detecting, identifying, and mitigating different kinds of attacks against Automatic Generation Control applications, which are used in power-grid systems to maintain frequencies at acceptable levels [103]. Work has also been done that examines the problem from a general or high-level perspective, by developing domain [71] or software [36] models to aid in attack detection and protection of critical infrastructure. In addition, contributions have been made that examine the problem from the attacker's perspective, through the use of general, competing interacting-network models [84].

However, to the best of our knowledge, the work in this chapter, which extends work from [82], presents the first approach that models the attacker's intent through specific, real-world capabilities that they wish to gain, via an iterative application of exploits. The attacker's activities are also driven by unconventional sources of information (specifically darknets in this case) and do not necessarily depend on information directly related to defender systems. Furthermore, the recent rise of darknet markets specializing in zero-day exploits allows us to integrate information unavailable to previous work.

7.8 Conclusion

In future work, we plan to examine the problem from the defender's perspective. Specifically, we aim to identify the set of vulnerabilities a defender must patch in order to deny the attacker a specific set of capabilities. We also plan to run more experiments that take into account additional data, specifically exploit-costs, gathered from exploit kits sold on darknet markets.

Extending this model and more tightly integrating into the larger data pipeline are some of the many problems that will be addressed going forward. In the next chapter, we survey several other challenges that warrant further research to better understand deepweb and darkweb cyber threat intelligence.

8

Conclusion

8.1 Introduction

In this chapter, we describe the unique challenges to the important problem of sociocultural modeling of cyber threat actors and why they necessitate further advances in artificial intelligence—particularly with regard to interdisciplinary efforts with the social sciences.

Cybersecurity is often referred to as "offense dominant" alluding to the notion that the domain generally favors the attacker [67]. The reasoning behind this is simple: a successful defense requires total control over all pathways to a system while a successful attack requires only one. As a result, any given cyber-defense based on the hardening of systems will fall prey to a cyber-attack as perpetrators gain knowledge and resources. Solutions have ranged from sophisticated adaptive defense strategies to offensive cyber-operations directed against malicious hackers. However, these methods have various technical shortcomings—which range from the technical immaturity of adaptive defenses to consequences of aggressive cyber-counteroperations. This process can lead to undesirable effects such as preemptive and preventative cyber war.

More and more, the cybersecurity industry has been moving toward the threat intelligence that we have been highlighting throughout the book, with the end goal being to preempt cyber-attacks before they occur. Discussed thoroughly in Chapter 3, a key source of cyber threat intelligence lies in the digital communities of malicious hackers—consisting of sites, markets, chat-rooms, and social media channels where information is shared, hackers are recruited, and the latest malware and exploits are bought and sold. Artificial intelligence and machine-learning techniques for analyzing communities on the Internet are long-established across specialty areas such as data-mining, information retrieval, and web science. However, we argue that the study of hacker communities combined with the goal of automating the collection and analysis of information about the activity of cyber threat actors, produces some very unique challenges. In this chapter, we describe some unique characteristics of cyber threat sociocultural environments and several challenging modeling problems for which various artificial intelligence techniques can be used to help solve.

8.2 Environmental Characteristics

When introducing hacker communities in Chapter 3, we studied them from a qualitative standpoint. We noted several unique characteristics in the online sociocultural environments frequented by malicious hackers that make these communities distinct from other groups. Some of these characteristics include the following.

- *Bounded anonymity.* Individuals participating in the malicious hacker community online make efforts to hide their identity. Some, however, seek to maintain a consistent online persona to gain social status in the hacker meritocracy.
- *Participation in high-risk behavior.* Despite recent arrests of individuals associated with darknet markets as well as suspicions of law-enforcement infiltration, many individuals still participate in discussions about illegal activities in darknet forums. Likewise, individuals participate in hacktivist operations advertised through social media. A recent lab-based behavioral study has explored some of the potential factors that would lead an individual to participate in risky hacktivism activities [14].
- *High incentives to cheat.* The existence of marketplaces where malicious hackers sell software and exploits to others is an environment where both parties are highly incentivized to cheat. For instance, the sale of a faulty product and violations of exclusive use agreements can be conducted with relative ease.
- *Ability to deceive.* The anonymous nature of these environments, combined with the fact that various aspects of a malicious hacker's digital persona can be forged, allows for deceptive activities to occur with relative ease.

These characteristics are interesting in several ways. First, from a sociological and behavioral standpoint, the freedom with which individuals in these communities discuss criminal activities, as well as share information and code with individuals likely involved with computer-related crimes (which itself is also a crime), begs the question how trust is afforded to enable observable social interactions. Second, characteristics such as anonymity and deception lead to modeling challenges—perhaps requiring consideration of latent attributes. Third, aspects such as cheating may actually constrain models to a degree—hence leading to model simplifications.

8.3 Challenges

In this section, we describe a few major challenges for modeling sociocultural cyber threat actor communities. Overcoming these challenges will provide new insights into this environment and also aid in higher-level tasks, such as predicting cyber-attacks and understanding the development of exploits and malware by these communities.

- *Establishment of social status in an anonymous environment.* In order for a malicious hacking community to exist, there must be anonymity, yet actors stand to gain from prestige earned in the hacker meritocracy, such as access to invite-only forums, trust in social interactions in general as opposed to undergoing frequent vetting processes. Modeling the accumulation of this latent quantity with proxy measurements is challenging in non-anonymous environments—and the level of anonymity itself creates even more difficult challenges. However, in addressing these challenges, we can better identify significant cyber threat actors and associate a greater degree of confidence with their actions. Recently, there has been some initial, descriptive work on this topic [1].
- *Data-driven modeling of risk-taking.* The adoption of risky behavior has gained attention in the computational social-science literature using model-based approaches [91]. However, instantiating models based on data remains largely an open question. The issue is further complicated by limited data on verified activities—as not all cyber-attacks are reported in the open. The goals in establishing such models for the study of cyber threats in determining when certain risky behavior will occur is likely to aid in prediction and preventative cyber defense.
- *Emergence and disintegration of trust-based communities.* For darknet marketplaces to thrive, populations of individuals have to make decisions to trust both those running the marketplace and many of the vendors. While there are established models for trust among individuals, understanding how the propagation of trust is initiated and spread in anonymous environments—which seem to discourage trust—remains an open question. By addressing this problem, we can better understand when a given cyber-exploit/malware marketplace will become well established.

- *Modeling deception hypotheses.* In order to properly attribute individual activity on the darknet to that seen in public in cases of cyber-attacks, or attributing the author of a given malware or exploit, cybersecurity analysts consider the "deception hypothesis." This approach considers the chance that some or all of the observed evidence was planted by an adversary. Therefore, for models designed for problems relating to cyber-attribution, we must also consider the deception hypothesis. In some of our ongoing efforts, we are leveraging defeasible logic programming to explicitly consider this approach.

8.4 Conclusion

In this book, after providing motivation for the use of cyber threat intelligence, we discussed online hacker community structure in detail and introduced data-mining and machine-learning techniques to digest large amounts of data from these communities. We then further analyzed this data and the structure of these hacker communities via unsupervised learning. Finally, we introduced models capable of leveraging this data to provide system-specific information with both a game theoretic host defense model and an industrial control system defense model. Through all of these applications, we hoped to illustrate the utility of cyber threat intelligence and demonstrate that systems with real-world value can be built.

There are still significant challenges to overcome in this area, including the modeling problems associated with the unique characteristics of the socio-cultural environment for cyber threat actors. Nevertheless, we believe that cyber threat intelligence gathering and its analysis will make up a significant portion of an organization's cyber defense posture in the not-too-distant future. Our ongoing work attempts to address some of the challenges discussed in this chapter, and we aim to further integrate all of the models and systems presented to provide real-time, system-specific threat intelligence. We believe this once hard-to-imagine proposal is attainable thanks to recent advances in the field.

Glossary

1337 Speak 1337 speak, pronounced "leetspeak," is an alternative way of spelling, which is characteristic of some hacker communities and involves replacing letters with numerals.

A* Search A path-finding algorithm from the Artificial Intelligence literature that leverages a heuristic function to generally improve performance over uninformed, brute-force searches. A* provides an optimal solution if the heuristic function is admissible.

Admissible Heuristic If a heuristic function in a path-finding algorithm never overestimates the remaining distance to a target, it is said to be admissible.

Bitcoin A popular crypto-currency that allows for the anonymous transfer of funds between parties.

Botnet A collection of infected computers that can be used in tandem for malicious purposes (e.g., DDoS attacks), typically without the owner's knowledge.

Co-training A semi-supervised learning technique in which two classifiers use a small number of labeled samples to try to infer the labels of a large set of unlabeled samples.

Crawler A program designed to traverse the website and retrieve HTML documents.

Crypto-currency Digital currency that leverages encryption and typically decentralized transactions in an attempt to anonymize transaction.

Darkweb The portion of the Internet accessible only when connected to anonymous communication services crypto-networks like Tor provides.

Deception Hypothesis A modeling approach that considers the chance that some or all of the observed evidence was planted by an adversary.

Deepweb Commonly refers to websites hosted on the open portion of the Internet (the "clearnet"), but not indexed by search engines [60].

Depth-First Search (DFS) An uninformed search algorithm from the Computer Science literature.

Distributed Denial of Service (DDoS) An attack in which a collection of infected computers (i.e., botnet) is used to flood a target with traffic in an attempt to disrupt service.

Escrow Service The process of having a third-party hold onto money during a transaction until the validity of the goods or services can be confirmed. This is a frequent practice on darknet markets.

Exploit A piece of software written to leverage a flaw in a different piece of software.

Hitting Set An NP-Complete problem that is a reformulation of Set Cover.

I2P A popular crypto-network, similar in nature to TOR.

Industrial Control System (ICS) IT infrastructure that controls physical systems (electricity, water, industrial machinery, etc.).

k-means clustering An algorithm used to partition a set of data points into k distinct subsets, where the points in each subset are close in some (usually euclidean) space.

Keylogger A piece of hardware or software used to record all key presses on a machine, often sending that information to a remote machine.

Label Propagation A semisupervised learning technique that assigns labels to unlabeled samples based on the unlabeled samples' similarity (based on some metric) to labeled samples.

Logistic Regression A classification algorithm that classifies samples by computing the odds ratio. The odds ratio gives the strength of association between the attributes and the class.

Moving Target Defense (MTD) A defense technique which aims to dynamically vary the attack surface that is presented to the attacker in order to make the discovery and exploitation of vulnerabilities more difficult.

NP-Complete A problem is NP-Complete if it is both NP-Hard and in NP.

NP-Hard A problem is NP-Hard if every problem in NP can be reduced to it in polynomial time.

Padonkaffsky Jargon Slang used predominantly in online Russian hacking communities.

Parser Software used to extract well-structured information from the HTML pages of marketplaces (regarding sale of malware/exploits) and hacker forums (discussion regarding services and threats).

Penetration Testing A proactive security technique designed to find vulnerabilities in a computer network or system.

Presented Attack Service In the context of system administration, the presented attack surface is the software that the sysadmin presents externally and that an attacker may interact with.

Rand Index A metric for determining cluster purity, defined as the number of pairs correctly considered in the same class or correctly considered in different classes divided by $\binom{n}{2}$, where n is the number of samples.

Random Forest An ensemble machine-learning method that combines bagging for each tree with random feature selection at each node to split the data, thus generating multiple decision tree classifiers. Each decision tree gives its own opinion on test sample classification. The prediction is made by taking a majority vote among the decision tree classifiers.

Remote Access Tool (RAT) Malicious RATs allow attackers to remotely take control of a machine, often with as much access as if they had physical access to the machine.

Semi-supervised Learning A class of machine learning in which target labels are known for only a subset of the training data, but the samples without labels are also used during training.

Set Cover A problem from the combinatorics literature that is one of the original NP-Complete problems. The problem is defined as given a set S, set $B \subseteq 2^S$ such that

$\bigcup_{b \in B} b = B$, and integer k, determine if there are k sets in B such that their union is S.

Supervised Learning Supervised learning is a technique in machine learning that is often, but not exclusively, used for classification problems. In supervised learning, a classification model is built with data that has ground-truth class labels (i.e., samples for which the true label is known). After the training period, the constructed model can be used to predict class labels for samples in which the ground-truth label is not known.

Support Vector Machine (SVM) A classification algorithm that works by finding a separating margin that maximizes the geometric distance between classes [29]. The separating margin is termed the hyperplane.

The Onion Router (TOR) Free software dedicated to protect the privacy of its users by obscuring traffic analysis as a form of network surveillance.

Unsupervised Learning A class of machine learning in which target labels are not used during the training phase.

Vulnerability A flaw in a piece of software.

Zero-day Exploits designed to leverage previously undiscovered vulnerabilities.

References

[1] Ahmed Abbasi, Weifeng Li, Victor Benjamin, Shiyu Hu, and Hsinchun Chen. Descriptive analytics: Examining expert hackers in web forums. In *IEEE – Joint Intelligence and Security Informatics Conference (JISIC)*, pp. 56–63. The Hague, The Netherlands, September 2014.

[2] Lillian Ablon, Martin C Libicki, and Andrea A Golay. *Markets for Cybercrime Tools and Stolen Data: Hackers' Bazaar*. Rand Corporation, 2014.

[3] Gunes Acar, Marc Juarez, Nick Nikiforakis, Claudia Diaz, Seda Gürses, Frank Piessens, and Bart Preneel. Fpdetective: Dusting the web for fingerprinters. In *Proceedings of the 2013 ACM SIGSAC Conference on Computer and Communications Security*, CCS '13, pp. 1129–1140, New York, NY, USA, 2013. ACM.

[4] Peter Apps. A cyber attack turned out the lights on 80,000. what can stop the next one?, 2016. http://blogs.reuters.com/great-debate/2016/04/05/a-cyber-attack-turned-out-the-lights-on-80000-what-can-stop-them/ (accessed October 6, 2016).

[5] Arma. Tor security advisory: Old tor browser bundles vulnerable. *The Tor Project*, August 2013. https://blog.torproject.org/blog/tor-security-advisory-old-tor-browser-bundles-vulnerable (accessed October 6, 2016).

[6] Yossi Azar and Iftah Gamzu. Efficient submodular function maximization under linear packing constraints. *ICALP*, 1:38–50, 2012.

[7] John A. Bargh and Katelyn Y. A. McKenna. The internet and social life. volume 55, pp. 573–590, 2004.

[8] Mikhail Belkin and Partha Niyogi. Using manifold structure for partially labelled classification. In *Advances in NIPS*, volume 15, pp. 929–936. MIT Press. 2003.

[9] Victor A. Benjamin, Weifeng Li, Thomas J. Holt, and Hsinchun Chen. Exploring threats and vulnerabilities in hacker web: Forums, irc, and carding shops. In *2015 International Conference on Intelligence and Security Informatics (IEEE)*, pp. 85–90, Baltimore, MD, USA, May 2015.

[10] Leyla Bilge and Tudor Dumitras. Before we knew it: an empirical study of zero-day attacks in the real world. In *Proceedings of the 2012 ACM conference on Computer and communications security*, pp. 833–844. ACM, 2012.

[11] Christopher M. Bishop and Ilkay Ulusoy. Object recognition via local patch labelling. In Joab Winkler, Mahesan Niranjan, Neil Lawrence, editors.

Deterministic and Statistical Methods in Machine Learning, pp. 1–21, Springer, Berlin, Heidelberg, 2005.

[12] David M Blei, Andrew Y Ng, and Michael I Jordan. Latent dirichlet allocation. *the Journal of Machine Learning Research*, 3:993–1022, 2003.

[13] Avrim Blum and Tom Mitchell. Combining labeled and unlabeled data with co-training. In *Proceedings of the Eleventh Annual Conference on Computational Learning Theory*, COLT' 98, pp. 92–100, New York, NY, USA, 1998. ACM.

[14] J. E. Bodford. *We Are Legion: Hacktivism as a Product of Deindividuation, Power, and Social Injustice*. PhD thesis, Arizona State University, 2015.

[15] Tom Boellstorff. *Coming of Age in Second Life: An Anthropologist Explores the Virtually Human*. Princeton University Press, Princeton, NJ, USA, 2008.

[16] Danny Bradbury. Unveiling the dark web. *Network Security*, volume 2014, pp. 14–17, 2014.

[17] Jeffrey Carr. *Inside Cyber Warfare: Mapping the Cyber Underworld*. O'Reilly Media, Inc. 2011.

[18] Soumen Chakrabarti, Kunal Punera, and Mallela Subramanyam. Accelerated focused crawling through online relevance feedback. In *Proceedings of the 11th International Conference on World Wide Web*, pp. 148–159. ACM, 2002.

[19] Soumen Chakrabarti, Martin Van den Berg, and Byron Dom. Focused crawling: a new approach to topic-specific web resource discovery. *Computer Networks*, 31(11):1623–1640, 1999.

[20] Hsinchun Chen. *Dark web: Exploring and Data Mining the Dark Side of the Web*, volume 30. Springer Science & Business Media, 2011.

[21] Hsinchun Chen, Wingyan Chung, Jialun Qin, Edna Reid, Marc Sageman, and Gabriel Weimann. Uncovering the dark web: A case study of jihad on the web. *Journal of the American Society for Information Science and Technology*, volume 59, pp. 1347–1359. 2008.

[22] Hong Cheng, Zicheng Liu, and Jie Yang 0001. Sparsity induced similarity measure for label propagation. In *2009 IEEE 12th International Conference on Computer Vision*, pp. 317–324. IEEE, 2009.

[23] Bill Chu, Thomas J. Holt, and Gail Joon Ahn. *Examining the Creation, Distribution, and Function of Malware On Line*. Washington, D.C., 2010. National Institute of Justice.

[24] E. Gabriella Coleman. Ethnographic approaches to digital media. *Annual Review of Anthropology*, volume 39, pp. 487–505, 2010.

[25] E. Gabriella Coleman. *Coding Freedom: The Ethics and Aesthetics of Hacking*. Princeton University Press, 2013.

[26] Mandiant Consulting. M-trends 2016 cyber security trends. 2016. https://www.fireeye.com/current-threats/annual-threat-report/mtrends.html (accessed October 6, 2016).

[27] Thomas H Cormen. *Introduction to Algorithms*. MIT Press, 2009.

[28] The MITRE Corporation. CVE-2009-1185, 2009.

[29] Corinna Cortes and Vladimir Vapnik. Support-vector networks. *Machine Learning*, volume 20, pp. 273–297, 1995.

[30] R. Dingledine, N. Mathewson, and P. Syverson. Tor: The second-generation onion router. In *Proceedings of the 13th Conference on USENIX Security Symposium use serial (Oxford) comma: x, y, and z)—Volume 13*, SSYM'04, pp. 21–21, 2004.

[31] Wim B. H. J. van de Donk (ed.). *Cyberprotest : New Media, Citizens, and Social Movements*. Routledge London; New York, 2004.

[32] David Fackler. N.S.A. breached North Korean networks before Sony attack, officials say, 2015. http://www.nytimes.com/2015/01/19/world/asia/nsa-tapped-into-north-korean-networks-before-sony-attack-officials-say.html (accessed October 6, 2016).

[33] Nicolas Falliere, Liam O Murchu, and Eric Chien. W32. stuxnet dossier. White paper, Symantec Corp., Security Response, 5, 2011.

[34] Uriel Feige. A threshold of ln n for approximating set cover. *J. ACM*, 45(4):634–652, July 1998.

[35] Jim Finkle. Cyber insurance premiums rocket after high-profile attacks, 2016. http://www.reuters.com/article/us-cybersecurity-insurance-insight-idUSKCN0S609M20151012 (accessed October 6, 2016).

[36] F Flammini, A Gaglione, N Mazzocca, and C Pragliola. Detect: a novel framework for the detection of attacks to critical infrastructures. *Safety, Reliability and Risk Analysis: Theory, Methods and Applications-Proceedings of ESREL'08*, pp. 105–112, 2014.

[37] Tianjun Fu, Ahmed Abbasi, and Hsinchun Chen. A focused crawler for dark web forums. *Journal of the American Society for Information Science and Technology*, 61(6):1213–1231, 2010.

[38] Yezekael Hayel and Quanyan Zhu. Resilient and secure network design for cyber attack-induced cascading link failures in critical infrastructures. In *Information Sciences and Systems (CISS), 2015 49th Annual Conference on*, pp. 1–3. IEEE, 2015.

[39] Thomas J. Holt. Lone hacks or group cracks: Examining the social organization of computer hackers. In Schmalleger, Frank J., and Michael Pittaro, editors, *Crimes of the Internet*, pp. 336–355. Prentice Hall Press, Upper Saddle River, NJ, USA, 1st edition, 2009.

[40] Thomas J. Holt and Bernadette H. Schell. *Hackers and Hacking: A Reference Handbook*. Contemporary World Issues. ABC-CLIO, LLC, 2013.

[41] Thomas J. Holt, Deborah Strumsky, Olga Smirnova, and Max Kilger. Examining the social networks of malware writers and hackers. *International Journal of Cyber Criminology*, volume 6, pp. 891–903, 2012.

[42] Thomas J. (ed.) Holt. *Crime On-Line—Correlates, Causes, and Context*. Caroline Academic Press, 2nd edition, 2013.

[43] Peter Holtz, Nicole Kronberger, and Wolfgang Wagner. Analyzing internet forums: A practical guide. *Journal of Media Psychology*, volume 24, pp. 55–66, 2012.

[44] Courtenay Honeycutt and Susan Herring. Beyond microblogging: Conversation and collaboration via twitter. *System Sciences, 2009. HICSS'09. 42nd Hawaii International Conference on*. IEEE, volume 42, pp. 1–10, 2009.

[45] Alice Hutchings and Thomas J. Holt. A crime script analysis of the online stolen data market. *British Journal of Criminology*, volume 55, pp. 596–614, 2014.

[46] K. Jaishankar. Space transition theory of cyber crimes. In Schmalleger, Frank J., and Michael Pittaro, editors, *Crimes of the Internet*, pp. 283–301. Prentice Hall Press, Upper Saddle River, NJ, USA, 1st edition, 2009.

[47] Sushil Jajodia, Anup K Ghosh, VS Subrahmanian, Vipin Swarup, Cliff Wang, and X Sean Wang. Moving target defense ii. *Application of Game Theory*

and Adversarial Modeling. Series: Advances in Information Security, 100:203, 2013.

[48] Sushil Jajodia, Anup K Ghosh, Vipin Swarup, Cliff Wang, and X Sean Wang. *Moving Target Defense: Creating Asymmetric Uncertainty for Cyber Threats*, volume 54. Springer Science & Business Media, 2011.

[49] Akshay Java, Xiaodan Song, Tim Finin, and Belle Tseng. Why we twitter: Understanding microblogging usage and communities. In *Proceedings of the 9th WebKDD and 1st SNA-KDD 2007 Workshop on Web Mining and Social Network Analysis*, WebKDD/SNA-KDD '07, pp. 56–65, New York, NY, USA, 2007. ACM.

[50] Robert E Johnson III. Survey of SCADA security challenges and potential attack vectors. In *Internet Technology and Secured Transactions (ICITST), 2010 International Conference for*, pp. 1–5. IEEE, 2010.

[51] Tim Jordan and Paul Taylor. A sociology of hackers. *The Sociological Review*, volume 46, pp. 757–780. Blackwell Publishing Ltd, 1998.

[52] Jeffrey S. Juris. Reflections on occupy everywhere: Social media, public space, and emerging logics of aggregation. *American Ethnologist*, 39(2):259–279, 2012.

[53] Stamatis Karnouskos. Stuxnet worm impact on industrial cyber-physical system security. In *IECON 2011-37th Annual Conference on IEEE Industrial Electronics Society*, pp. 4490–4494. IEEE, 2011.

[54] Swati Khandelwal. Malware and hacking forum seized, dozens arrested. July 2015. http://thehackernews.com/2015/07/darkode-hacking-forum.html (accessed October 6, 2016). http://thehackernews.com/2016/01/MegalodonHTTP-DDoS-Botnet.html (accessed October 6, 2016).

[55] Swati Khanderwal. Creator of megalodonhttp ddos botnet arrested. January 2016. http://thehackernews.com/2016/01/MegalodonHTTP-DDoS-Botnet.html (accessed October 6, 2016).

[56] Christopher Kiekintveld, Viliam Lisý, and Radek Píbil. Game-theoretic foundations for the strategic use of honeypots in network security. In Sushil Jajodia, Paulo Shakarian ,V.S. Subrahmanian, Vipin Swarup, Cliff Wang, editors, *Cyber Warfare—Building the Scientific Foundation*, Springer International Publishing, pp. 81–101. 2015.

[57] Bronislaw Knaster and A Tarski. Un théoreme sur les fonctions d'ensembles. *Ann. Soc. Polon. Math*, 6(133):2013134, 1928.

[58] Robert V. Kozinets. *Netnography: Doing Ethnographic Research Online*. Sage Publications Ltd., 2009.

[59] Brian Krebs. Target hackers broke in via hvac company—Krebs on security, 2016. https://krebsonsecurity.com/2014/02/target-hackers-broke-in-via-hvac-company/ (accessed October 6, 2016).

[60] David Lacey and Paul M. Salmon. It's dark in there: Using systems analysis to investigate trust and engagement in dark web forums. In D. Harris, editor, *Engineering Psychology and Cognitive Ergonomics*, volume 9174 of *Lecture Notes in Computer Science*, pp. 117–128. Springer International Publishing, 2015.

[61] Jure Leskovec, Andreas Krause, Carlos Guestrin, Christos Faloutsos, Jeanne VanBriesen, and Natalie Glance. Cost-effective outbreak detection in networks. In *Proceedings of the 13th ACM SIGKDD International Conference on Knowledge Discovery and Data Mining*, pp. 420–429. ACM, 2007.

[62] Anat Levin, Dani Lischinski, and Yair Weiss. A closed form solution to natural image matting. In *Proceedings of the 2006 IEEE Computer Society Conference on Computer Vision and Pattern Recognition—Volume 1*, CVPR '06, pp. 61–68, Washington, DC, USA, 2006. IEEE Computer Society.

[63] Steven Levy. *Hackers: Heroes of the Computer Revolution*. Doubleday, New York, NY, USA, 1984.

[64] Weifeng Li and Hsinchun Chen. Identifying top sellers in underground economy using deep learning-based sentiment analysis. In *Intelligence and Security Informatics Conference (JISIC), 2014 IEEE Joint*, pp. 64–67, Sept 2014.

[65] Andrea Locatelli. The offense/defense balance in cyberspace. *ISPI Analysis*, No. 203, October 2013.

[66] Kong-wei Lye and Jeannette M Wing. Game strategies in network security. *International Journal of Information Security*, 4(1):71–86, 2005.

[67] William J Lynn III. Defending a new domain. *Foreign Affairs*, 89(5):97–108, 2010.

[68] Mitch Macdonald, Richard Frank, Joseph Mei, and Bryan Monk. Identifying digital threats in a hacker web forum. In *Proceedings of the 2015 IEEE/ACM International Conference on Advances in Social Networks Analysis and Mining 2015*, ASONAM '15, pp. 926–933, New York, NY, USA, 2015. ACM.

[69] D. E. Mann and S. M. Christey. Towards a Common Enumeration of Vulnerabilities, 1999. http://www.cve.mitre.org/docs/docs-2000/cerias.html (accessed October 6, 2016).

[70] Ericsson Marin, Ahmad Diab, and Paulo Shakarian. Product offerings in malicious hacker markets. *IEEE Conference on Intelligence and Security Informatics (ISI-16)*, 2016.

[71] Stefano Marrone, Roberto Nardone, Annarita Tedesco, Pasquale D'Amore, Valeria Vittorini, Roberto Setola, Francesca De Cillis, and Nicola Mazzocca. Vulnerability modeling and analysis for critical infrastructure protection applications. *International Journal of Critical Infrastructure Protection*, 6(3):217–227, 2013.

[72] Martha McCaughey and Michael D. Ayers, editors. *Cyberactivism: Online Activism in Theory and Practice*. Taylor and Francis, Inc., Bristol, PA, USA, 2003.

[73] H Brendan McMahan, Geoffrey J Gordon, and Avrim Blum. Planning in the presence of cost functions controlled by an adversary. In *Proceedings of the Twentieth International Conference On Machine Learning*, pp. 536–543, 2003.

[74] Joseph Mei and Richard Frank. Sentiment crawling: Extremist content collection through a sentiment analysis guided web-crawler. In *Proceedings of the 2015 IEEE/ACM International Conference on Advances in Social Networks Analysis and Mining 2015*, pp. 1024–1027. ACM, 2015.

[75] Filippo Menczer, Gautam Pant, and Padmini Srinivasan. Topical web crawlers: Evaluating adaptive algorithms. *ACM Transactions on Internet Technology (TOIT)*, 4(4):378–419, 2004.

[76] Michel Minoux. Accelerated greedy algorithms for maximizing submodular set functions. In J. Stoer, editor, *Optimization Techniques*, volume 7 of *Lecture Notes in Control and Information Sciences*, pp. 234–243. Springer Berlin Heidelberg, 1978.

[77] Marti Motoyama, Damon McCoy, Kirill Levchenko, Stefan Savage, and Geoffrey M. Voelker. An analysis of underground forums. In *Proceedings of the 2011 ACM SIGCOMM Conference on Internet Measurement Conference*, IMC '11, pp. 71–80. ACM, New York, NY, USA, 2011.

[78] G.L. Nemhauser, L.A. Wolsey, and M.L. Fisher. An analysis of approximations for maximizing submodular set functions. *Mathematical Programming*, 14(1):265–294, 1978.

[79] Kien C Nguyen, Tansu Alpcan, and Tamer Başar. Stochastic games for security in networks with interdependent nodes. In *Game Theory for Networks, 2009. GameNets' 09. International Conference on*, pp. 697–703. IEEE, 2009.

[80] Eric Nunes, Ahmad Diab, Andrew Gunn, Ericsson Marin, Vineet Mishra, Vivin Paliath, John Robertson, Jana Shakarian, Amanda Thart, and Paulo Shakarian. Darknet and deepnet mining for proactive cybersecurity threat intelligence. *IEEE Conference on Intelligence and Security Informatics (ISI-16)*, 2016.

[81] Federal Bureau of Investigation. Cyber criminal forum taken down—members arrested in 20 countries, July 2015. https://www.fbi.gov/news/stories/cyber-criminal-forum-taken-down (accessed October 6, 2016).

[82] Vivin Paliath and Paulo Shakarian. Modeling cyber-attacks on industrial control systems. *IEEE Conference on Intelligence and Security Informatics (ISI-16)*, 2016.

[83] Ben Plesser. Skilled, cheap Russian hackers power American cybercrime. *NBC News*, February 2014.

[84] Boris Podobnik, Davor Horvatic, Tomislav Lipic, Matjaz Perc, Javier M Buldu, and H Eugene Stanley. The cost of attack in competing networks. *Journal of The Royal Society Interface*, 12(112):20150770, 2015.

[85] John Postill and Sarah Pink. Social media ethnographie: The digital researcher in a messy web. *Media International Australia*, volume 145, pp. 123–134, 2012.

[86] Andrew Quodling. Doxxing, swatting and the new trends in online harassment. *The Conversation*, April 2015.

[87] William M. Rand. Objective Criteria for the Evaluation of Clustering Methods. *Journal of the American Statistical Association*, 66(336):846–850, December 1971.

[88] Michael Rausch, Nathan Good, and Chris J. Hoofnagle. Searching for indicators of device fingerprinting in the javascript code of popular websites. *Proceedings, Midwest Instruction and Computing Symposium*, 2014.

[89] John Robertson, Ahmad Diab, Ericsson Marin, Eric Nunes, Vivin Paliath, Jana Shakarian, and Paulo Shakarian. Darkweb mining and game theory for enhanced cyber threat intelligence. *The Cyber Defense Review*, volume 2, 2016.

[90] John Robertson, Vivin Paliath, Jana Shakarian, Amanda Thart, and Paulo Shakarian. Data driven game theoretic cyber threat mitigation. In *Proc. 28th Innovative Applications of Artificial Intelligence (IAAI-16)*, 2016.

[91] Patrick Roos, J Ryan Carr, and Dana S Nau. Evolution of state-dependent risk preferences. *ACM Transactions on Intelligent Systems and Technology (TIST)*, 1(1):6, 2010.

[92] Sagar Samtani, Ryan Chinn, and Hsinchun Chen. Exploring hacker assets in underground forums. *Intelligence and Security Informatics (ISI), 2015 IEEE International Conference on*. IEEE, pp. 31–36, May 2015.

[93] Jana Shakarian, Paulo Shakarian, and Andrew Ruef. Cyber-attacks and public embarrassment: A survey of some notable hacks. *Elsevier SciTechConnect*, 2015. https://www.researchgate.net/publication/271217696_Cyber_Attacks_and_Public_Embarrassment_A_Survey_of_Some_Notable_Hacks (accessed October 6, 2016).

[94] P. Shakarian and J. Shakarian. Considerations for the development of threat prediction in the cyber domain. *AAAI Workshop on Artificial Intelligence for Cyber Security (AICS)*, 2015.

[95] P. Shakarian, J. Shakarian, and A. Ruef. *Introduction to Cyber-Warfare: A Multidisciplinary Approach*. Elsevier Science, 2013.

[96] Paulo Shakarian. The 2008 Russian cyber-campaign against Georgia. *Military Review*, volume 91, Nov.-Dec., p. 63, 2011.

[97] Paulo Shakarian. Stuxnet: Cyberwar revolution in military affairs. *Small Wars Journal*, April 2011. http://smallwarsjournal.com/jrnl/art/stuxnet-cyberwar-revolution-in-military-affairs (accessed October 6, 2016).

[98] Paulo Shakarian, Hansheng Lei, and Roy Lindelauf. Power grid defense against malicious cascading failure. In *Proceedings of the 2014 international conference on Autonomous agents and multi-agent systems*, pp. 813–820. International Foundation for Autonomous Agents and Multiagent Systems, 2014.

[99] Paulo Shakarian and J. Shakarian. Considerations for the development of threat prediction in the cyber domain. In *AAAI-16 Workshop on Artificial Intelligence for Cyber Security*, 2016.

[100] Paulo Shakarian and Jana Shakarian. Socio-cultural modeling for cyber threat actors. In *Workshops at the Thirtieth AAAI Conference on Artificial Intelligence*, 2016.

[101] Jeffrey G. Snodgrass. Ethnography of online cultures. In Bernard, H. Russell, and Clarence C. Gravlee, editors, *Handbook of Methods in Cultural Anthropology*, pp. 465–496. Rowman and Littlefield, London, UK, 2015.

[102] Kyle Soska and Nicolas Christin. Measuring the longitudinal evolution of the online anonymous marketplace ecosystem. In *24th USENIX Security Symposium (USENIX Security 15)*, pp. 33–48, Washington, D.C., August 2015. USENIX Association.

[103] Siddharth Sridhar and Manimaran Govindarasu. Model-based attack detection and mitigation for automatic generation control. *Smart Grid, IEEE Transactions on*, 5(2):580–591, 2014.

[104] Kevin F. Steinmetz. Craft(y)ness: An ethnographic study of hacking. *British Journal of Criminology*, 55(1):125–145, 2015.

[105] Kevin F. Steinmetz and Jurgen Gerber. "It doesn't have to be this way": Hacker perspectives on privacy. 41(3):29–51, 2015.

[106] L. Stouffer, V. Pilitteri, S. Lightman, M. Abrams, and A. Hahn. Guide to industrial control systems (ICS) security, *NIST special publication* 800.82, pp. 16–16, 2011.

[107] Milind Tambe. *Security and Game Theory: Algorithms, Deployed Systems, Lessons Learned*. Cambridge University Press, New York, NY, USA, 1st edition, 2011.

[108] Andrew S. Tanenbaum and David J. Wetherall. *Computer Networks*. Prentice Hall Press, Upper Saddle River, NJ, USA, 5th edition, 2010.

[109] Paul A. Taylor. From hackers to hacktivists: speed bumps on the global super-highway? *New Media and Society*, 7(5):625–646, 2005.

[110] Robert W. Taylor, Eric J. Fritsch, and John Liederbach. *Digital Crime and Digital Terrorism*. Prentice Hall Press, 3rd edition, 2014.

[111] Sherry Turkle. *The Second Self: Computers and the Human Spirit*. Simon and Schuster, Inc., New York, NY, USA, 1984.

[112] US-CERT. GNU Bourne-Again Shell (Bash) "Shellshock" Vulnerability (CVE-2014-6271, CVE-2014-7169, CVE-2014-7186, CVE-2014-7187, CVE-2014-6277 and CVE-2014-6278), 2014.

[113] Dan S. Wall. *Cybercrime: The Transformation of Crime in the Information Age*. Polity, 1st edition, 2007.

[114] Changhu Wang, Shuicheng Yan, Lei Zhang 0001, and Hong-Jiang Zhang. Multi-label sparse coding for automatic image annotation. In *Computer Vision and Pattern Recognition, 2009. CVPR 2009. IEEE Conference on*, pp. 1643–1650. IEEE, 2009.

[115] Wang Wei. Hunting Russian malware author behind Phoenix exploit kit. April 2013. http://thehackernews.com/2013/04/hunting-russian-malware-author-behind.html (accessed October 6, 2016).

[116] Bryce Westlake, Martin Bouchard, and Richard Frank. Assessing the validity of automated webcrawlers as data collection tools to investigate online child sexual exploitation. *Sexual Abuse: A Journal of Research and Treatment*, pp. 1–24, 2015.

[117] Kyle Wilhoit. Killdisk and blackenergy are not just energy sector threats—trendlabs security intelligence blog, 2016. http://blog.trendmicro.com/trendlabs-security-intelligence/killdisk-and-blackenergy-are-not-just-energy-sector-threats/ (accessed October 6, 2016).

[118] Ziming Zhao, Gail-Joon Ahn, Hongxin Hu, and Deepinder Mahi. Socialimpact: Systematic analysis of underground social dynamics. In Sara Foresti, Moti Yung, and Fabio Martinelli, editors, *ESORICS*, volume 7459 of *Lecture Notes in Computer Science*, pp. 877–894. Springer, 2012.

[119] Xiaojin Zhu, John Lafferty, and Zoubin Ghahramani. Combining active learning and semi-supervised learning using gaussian fields and harmonic functions. In *ICML 2003 Workshop on The Continuum from Labeled to Unlabeled Data in Machine Learning and Data Mining*, pp. 58–65, 2003.

Index